The Vampire Library

# Vampires
# in the Movies

ADAM WOOG

ReferencePoint
Press®

San Diego, CA

*For Stephanie Wichmann and Mary Alice Tully, my favorite vampire fans.*

## About the Author

Adam Woog has written many books for adults, young adults, and children. He and his wife live in Seattle, Washington. They have a daughter who is in college.

**For more information, contact:**
ReferencePoint Press, Inc.
PO Box 27779
San Diego, CA 92198
www.ReferencePointPress.com

Picture credits:
Cover: iStockphoto.com
Fortean Picture Library: 6
iStockphoto.com: 14, 41
Photofest: 10, 19, 26, 31, 49, 52, 56, 60, 66, 70


Series design and book layout: Amy Stirnkorb

LIBRARY OF CONGRESS CATALOGING-IN-PUBLICATION DATA

Woog, Adam, 1953-
  Vampires in the movies / by Adam Woog.
    p. cm. -- (The vampire library series)
  Includes bibliographical references and index.
  ISBN-13: 978-1-60152-135-4 (hardback)
  ISBN-10: 1-60152-135-9 (hardback)
  1. Vampire films--History and criticism--Juvenile literature. I. Title.
  PN1995.9.V3W66 2010
  791.43'675--dc22
                                                         2010017982

# Contents

Introduction: Blood-Sucking Stars of the Silver Screen     4

Chapter 1: Dawn of the Movie Undead     8

Chapter 2: The Vampire Evolves     22

Chapter 3: Blockbusters and Other Twists
         on an Immortal Tale     35

Chapter 4: The Building Blocks of Vampire Flicks     50

Chapter 5: Breaking the Mold     63

Source Notes     76

For Further Exploration     77

Index     78

# Introduction

# Blood-Sucking Stars of the Silver Screen

Vampires, those bloodthirsty creatures of the night, have been staples of horror movies since the dawn of filmmaking. Many of the older movies seem quaint to modern viewers—corny, with poor acting and crude special effects. But even the creakiest silent movie was an exciting and revolutionary new form of art and entertainment in its day. Likewise, even the cheesiest gore-fest from later years was just a reflection of what was popular and stylish at the time. More than a century after a vampire first stalked across the silver screen, bloodsuckers remain some of the most enduring figures in film—some might even say they are immortal.

## Vlad the Impaler

Legends of undead creatures who live forever, feed on the blood of humans, and sometimes make their victims into vampires as well have existed for thousands of years and in cultures from all over the world. For example, writings from ancient Babylon mention such creatures. But the most famous vampire legend, a direct ancestor of the most famous movie vampire, comes from a part of eastern Europe called Transylvania, in what is now Romania.

Ancient stories from there tell of a fifteenth-century aristocrat called Vlad Tepes, also known as Vlad Dracul. According to these legends, he was a bloodthirsty and sadistic warrior-ruler who liked to kill his enemies in several grisly ways, including impaling them on sharpened pikes and leaving the bodies to rot—hence his nickname, Vlad the Impaler.

He was a real person and really did kill countless people, but there is no hard evidence that the ruler was a vampire. He remained an obscure footnote to history until 1897, when an Irish novelist, Bram Stoker, used his name and legend for a book that has become synonymous with bloodcurdling shivers. This book, of course, was *Dracula*.

Strange as it Sounds...

Dracula is the most-portrayed monster in film history.

## *Dracula* the Novel

Stoker's book begins with Jonathan Harker, an English lawyer, traveling to Castle Dracula in the rugged mountains of Transylvania and Moldavia. He is carrying papers for the reclusive Count Dracula, who is buying property in England.

Harker is first charmed by Dracula, but soon realizes that he is being held captive—and that his host is a vampire. Harker manages to escape. Meanwhile, as he rushes home, a sailing ship carrying a cargo of coffins filled with dirt crashes on the coast of England. All of the ship's crew is dead from some mysterious disease, and a strange creature is seen leaping from the ship to the land.

Soon after this occurs, Dracula travels to London, where he meets Harker's fiancée Mina Murray, her friend Lucy

*Villagers impaled on sharp wooden stakes suffer a gruesome death while the corpses of their neighbors are chopped into pieces in preparation for roasting. In the middle of it all, Vlad the Impaler feasts.*

Westenra, and Dr. John Seward, who works in an insane asylum. Lucy falls ill, and mysterious bite marks are found on her neck. Puzzled, Seward consults his friend Professor

Abraham Van Helsing, an expert on infectious diseases, and Van Helsing realizes that a vampire has bitten her. Lucy dies and is buried, but soon she returns to hunt children by night for their blood. Van Helsing enlists Seward and Harker (who by now has returned home) to help hunt her. They manage to kill Lucy by driving a wooden stake through her heart and cutting her head off.

But the Count is not through. He attacks Mina (now Mrs. Harker) and feeds his own blood to her, which makes her a semivampire and connects her telepathically with him. Dracula then heads back to Transylvania. The tracking party follows the Count to his castle, where the humans manage to kill the vampire by stabbing him in the heart and neck. As Dracula crumbles to dust, Mina is freed from his spell.

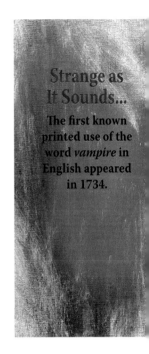

**Strange as It Sounds...**

The first known printed use of the word *vampire* in English appeared in 1734.

## Perennial Favorites

Stoker's novel was a huge success, thanks to its shivery thrills and such potent themes as the uncertainty of life after death, rebirth, and the temptations of evil. Terence Fisher, who directed many of the most popular vampire movies ever made, points out, "The whole idea of evil is very attractive."[1]

It is not surprising, therefore, that *Dracula* immediately became a hit stage play and, since the medium's earliest days, a perennial theme in the movies. The Internet Movie Data Base lists over 200 entries just for films that feature Dracula characters—and that does not count the many non-Dracula vampire flicks. According to the same source, more than 60 vampire movies are scheduled for release in 2010 alone. No wonder that the *Guinness Book of World Records* lists Dracula as the character most frequently portrayed in horror films. Clearly, vampires and movies are a match, you might say, made in heaven.

# Chapter 1

# Dawn of the Movie Undead

**M**ovie monsters rose up at the motion picture era's first light of dawn. It was 1896, to be precise, only a year after Bram Stoker published his now-famous book.

The two-minute movie *Le manoir du diable* (*The Devil's Castle)* is not really a vampire movie. It is worth mentioning, however, because it was the world's first horror film. The man who conjured it up was Georges Méliès, a French pioneer of the film industry. In his crude film, a huge bat turns into a devil—but a brave soldier holds up a cross and banishes it.

## The First Vampire Movies

Silent movies were immediate smash sensations with the public, and as their popularity expanded so did their subject matter. As far as is known, the first film that was unmistakably about vampires appeared in 1916: a German movie called *Nachte de Grauens* (*Night of Terror*). It remains a tantalizing mystery, however. No prints exist, and little is known about it or its American-born creator Arthur Robison.

*Nachte de Grauens* makes no mention of the name "Dracula." The first to do so, as far as film scholars know, was a 1921 Hungarian film, *Drakula halála* (*The Death of Drac-*

*ula*). As with the earlier film, no prints are known to exist; apparently, only a few publicity photos survive.

Director Károly Lajthay shot *Drakula halála* in Austria and Hungary. It is based only very loosely on Stoker's novel. The details differ depending on the source, but all agree that the film tells the story of a woman who either visits or is committed to an insane asylum. An inmate who claims to be Dracula haunts her dreams there. She later marries but remains plagued by visions of the vampire, unsure which parts of her life are real and which are hallucinations.

## The First Classic

In 1922, soon after the Hungarian film was shot, the first genuine vampire classic was released: *Nosferatu*. (Its full title was *Nosferatu, eine Symphonie des Grauens*—or *Nosferatu: A Symphony of Terror*.)

The movie's director was F.W. Murnau, one of the great masters of an artistic style called German Expressionism. Expressionism emphasizes wild emotions, deep shadows, and bizarre set designs. The best of the Expressionist films, including *Nosferatu*, are disturbing visions of madness and horror.

The filmmakers wanted to adapt Stoker's novel but could not acquire the rights, so they hired writer Henrik Galeen to write a screenplay using the same basic plot. Galeen set his story mainly in a fictional town in Germany and invented new names for the characters. Count Dracula became Count Orlok, Jonathan Harker became Thomas Hutter, and Mina Harker became Ellen Hutter. (The screenwriter eliminated the character of Van Helsing completely.)

Hutter travels to Count Orlok's castle to deliver papers for a house the Count is buying in Hutter's town. Stopping for the

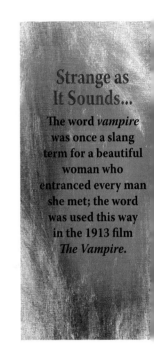

*The first genuine vampire classic, Nosferatu, was released in 1922. Done in the German Expressionist style, it presented a disturbing vision of madness and horror as can be seen in actor Max Schreck's portrayal of the title character (pictured).*

night en route, the businessman meets local residents who are terrified at the mention of Orlok's name; they relate the legend of a vampire called Nosferatu. Unafraid, Hutter continues to the castle and is greeted by the grotesque Count.

## Defeated by the Pure of Heart

As Hutter eats a late dinner, he accidentally cuts his thumb. Orlok wildly tries to suck the blood, but the young man pulls away in disgust. Later, when signing the papers, Orlok admires a picture of Hutter's wife—especially her lovely neck. Hutter starts to suspect that Orlok is Nosferatu, the vampire that terrified the villagers.

The next day, Hutter sees Orlok piling coffins onto a coach

and leaving. Hutter flees the castle but is injured and must recover before heading home. Meanwhile, Orlok loads his coffins—which are filled with soil and rats—onto a ship and sets sail for Hutter's town. En route, the ship's sailors sicken and die of plague carried by the rats, while Orlok sleeps in his coffin. After the Count docks the ship himself, the plague devastates the countryside.

Hutter returns, and Ellen realizes that the plague is connected to the Count. From a book about vampires, she learns that the only way to kill Orlok is for a pure-hearted woman to willingly surrender. He will lose track of time, and when the sun rises he will die.

When Orlok breaks into her bedroom, Ellen allows him to drink her blood, and, sated, he forgets about time. As the light of dawn hits him, the wicked Count disappears in a cloud of smoke. Ellen lives only long enough to be embraced by her grieving husband.

## Was Max Schreck a Real Vampire?

*Nosferatu* was shot in three locales: the German port city of Wismar, a studio in Berlin, and the ruins of a thirteenth-century structure, Orava Castle, in what is now Slovakia. The technology was crude by today's standards, and the single camera was cranked by hand. Nonetheless, Murnau created an atmosphere that is still unnerving.

The director was helped in fulfilling his vision by his perfectionist nature, which led him to painstakingly prepare every shot and even use a metronome to keep the pace of the acting flowing smoothly. For the most part, Murnau closely followed the detailed instructions that Galeen had specified in his screenplay. These included notes on camera positioning, lighting, and stage direction. The exception to this was the final scene, in which Orlok dies. Murnau rewrote this finale himself.

Perhaps the most striking aspect of *Nosferatu*, however, is the performance of the actor playing Orlok, a relative unknown named Max Schreck. *Schreck* is the German word for *fright*, and one theory is that he was a famous actor using a pseudonym. This cannot be proven, however, since Schreck's makeup makes it impossible to see his real face.

This makeup shows Orlok as a terrifying demon with long fingers and nails, a bald skull, sharp ratlike teeth, and pointed ears. Schreck was alleged to be a deeply strange person when not on screen, and—judging from his portrayal of the vampire—this is easy to believe. There were even rumors at the time that the actor was, in fact, a real vampire.

When the eagerly anticipated movie premiered at the Berlin Zoo in March 1922, guests were asked to wear fancy dress, meant to evoke the film's 1830s-era setting. *Nosferatu* opened to the public later that month and was a huge hit. However, trouble lay ahead for the filmmakers.

The changes made to Stoker's story were not enough to disguise *Nosferatu*'s origins. The novelist's widow sued, and the filmmakers declared bankruptcy. Florence Stoker pursued the matter, and a judge ordered all copies of the film destroyed. Fortunately for fans of classic movies, however, five prints survived. Their quality is imperfect, but they are good enough for the very creepy Count Orlok to still give audiences shivers.

## Dracula Goes to Hollywood

The first vampire "talkie"—that is, a movie with sound— was *Vampyr*, released in 1931. Its chief creator was a distinguished Danish writer/director, Carl Theodor Dreyer. Many

# "Extraordinary Pallor"

The original Dracula—the one Bram Stoker invented in his classic nineteenth-century novel—is quite unlike most of the characters portrayed in movies. Although his appearance grows younger as he drinks the blood of more victims, here is how he appears to Jonathan Harker, one of the characters in the book:

> His face was a strong—a very strong—aquiline, with high bridge of the thin nose and peculiarly arched nostrils; with lofty domed forehead, and hair growing scantily round the temples, but profusely elsewhere. His eyebrows were very massive, almost meeting over the nose, and with bushy hair that seemed to curl in its own profusion.
>
> The mouth, so far as I could see it under the heavy moustache, was fixed and rather cruel looking, with peculiarly sharp white teeth; these protruded over the lips, whose remarkable ruddiness showed astonishing vitality in a man of his years. For the rest, his ears were pale and at the tops extremely pointed; the chin was broad and strong, and the cheeks firm though thin. The general effect was one of extraordinary pallor.

Bram Stoker, *Dracula*. New York: Cosimo, 2009, p. 15.

*Slovakia's Orava Castle (shown here under a dusting of winter snow) is one of three locations in Europe where the movie* Nosferatu *was filmed.*

film historians consider *Vampyr* a better film than *Nosferatu* and other, more famous early versions of the Dracula story. It is a dreamlike movie based on a collection of horror stories by writer Joseph Sheridan Le Fanu. It tells the story of a man in a remote country inn who believes he is surrounded by vampires—and then dreams of his own death and burial.

However, *Vampyr* was completely overshadowed by a film released the same year—the most famous vampire movie of all time. This was the film that was destined to make the blood-sucking Count Dracula into an icon, fixing a permanent place in cinema history for the voice, manner, and face of a particular actor. The film, of course, was *Dracula*.

This version was, by the standards of the time, a big-budget production (it cost $355,000, roughly $5 million in today's dollars), and this time it could legally use the Count's name. Universal Pictures in Hollywood had acquired the rights to a hugely popular stage version of *Dracula*, so with the permission of the Stoker estate the studio was free to adapt the novel without disguise.

Objections arose at first, however, because the play repelled many at Universal. One reader (a person who recommends or rejects scripts) commented, "While this may have a fantastic [run on stage] and be very engrossing for those who like the weird, I cannot possibly see how it is going to make a motion picture. It is blood—blood—blood—kill and everything that would cause any average human being to revolt. . . . Sorry but I cannot see that there is anything in this." Another reader added: "We all like to see ugly things . . . we are all attracted, to a certain extent, to that which is hideous . . . but when it passes a certain point, the attraction dies and we suffer a feeling of repulsion and nausea."[2]

Undaunted, the head of Universal, Carl Laemmle Jr., hired screenwriter Garrett Fort and director Tod Browning for the project. (Browning also made, among others, the classic horror picture *Freaks*.) For their lead actor, meanwhile, Universal turned to an actor with long experience in playing the Count.

His name was Béla Ferenc Dezső Blaskó. Born in the town of Lugos, in what is now Romania, he later adapted his hometown's name as his stage name. As Béla Lugosi, the actor moved to America, learned English, and became a star with the stage version of *Dracula*. The studio was able to hire him for a flat fee of $3,500.

## "I Never Drink . . . *Wine*"

Lugosi's version of the blood-sucking Count was miles from Max Schreck's disturbing and grotesque vampire. The Hungarian actor's take was smooth, seductive, and charming. His performance was dramatically aided by recent improvements in filmmaking, notably the revolutionary new technology of sound. *Dracula* was made during the time when "talkies" were replacing silent movies, so audiences could thrill to Lugosi's exotic and hypnotic voice.

The plot of *Dracula* loosely follows the novel (and, to a degree, *Nosferatu*). It begins with an Englishman named Renfield journeying to Transylvania with papers for Dracula's purchase of a house. The Transylvanian peasants are frightened of the night, warn Renfield about vampires, and give him a crucifix for protection. Film scholar Gregory A. Waller comments, "With this young traveler we encounter a land in which the terrified, pious, superstitious human beings live in a state of constant watchfulness."[3]

When the Count welcomes Renfield to his forbidding home, they hear wolves howling in the distance, and Dracula utters some now-famous lines: "Listen to them. Children of the night. What music they make!" He then offers Renfield a meal, explaining that he will not join his guest. Before Renfield begins to eat, his host utters the immortal words: "I never drink . . . *wine*."[4]

Dracula later attacks Renfield, beginning the process of making him a vampire. By the time they board a ship to England, Renfield is Dracula's slave; by the time they dock in London, the Englishman is the only living person on board. Browning, the film's director, makes an off-screen appearance here as the voice of the harbormaster who finds Renfield in the hold. He cries, "Why, he's mad—look at his eyes—the man's gone crazy."[5]

**Strange as It Sounds...**

The 1922 version of *Nosferatu* was banned in Sweden until 1972 because it was deemed too horrifying.

## Dracula Meets His End

Renfield is sent to a lunatic asylum, while the Count leaves his coffin and moves to his new home. There he befriends John Harker, Harker's fiancée Mina, and their friend Lucy Weston. Mina is a typical woman of the era, carefully protected from danger by men, in this case Harker and her father, Dr. Seward, who runs the lunatic asylum. Lucy, on the other hand, is far more independent—but also more vulnerable to the charms of the Count. That night Dracula appears as a bat, enters Lucy's bedroom, and gorges on her blood. She dies the next day, and doctors notice two puncture wounds on her neck. Dracula then visits Mina as she sleeps and bites her neck as well.

Meanwhile, Harker's friend, a scientist named Abraham Van Helsing (played by Edward Van Sloan, who had appeared with Lugosi on stage), examines Renfield. The madman is obsessed with eating insects, convinced that this will make him stronger. He also says that his master has promised him thousands of rats, and Van Helsing realizes that a vampire is on the loose—namely, the Count. His secret discovered, Dracula flees and, finding Mina, attacks her. The next morning, clearly ill, she is put to bed. Meanwhile, a newspaper reports that a beautiful woman in white has been attacking children in the park. This is Lucy, now transformed into a vampire.

Van Helsing enlists Harker and Seward to help him find the fiend, explaining that Dracula can be killed by driving a wooden stake into his heart. When the professor tracks him down, Dracula tries to hypnotize him but Van Helsing wards him off with a crucifix. Meanwhile, Mina, who is slowly becoming a vampire, attacks Harker.

Van Helsing and Seward arrive just in time to save

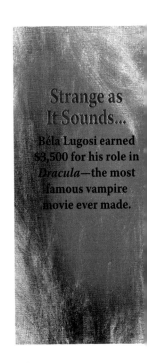

**Strange as It Sounds...**

Béla Lugosi earned $3,500 for his role in *Dracula*—the most famous vampire movie ever made.

Harker, but Dracula takes Mina captive and retreats to his coffin before sunrise. When the vampire killers catch up, Mina is nearly dead, but Van Helsing is able to kill Renfield and Dracula—at which time Mina returns to the living. She and Harker walk away together, leaving Van Helsing and Seward with the corpses.

## Audiences Faint from Fear

*Dracula* had some problems in production. Most important, all of the set-building, costumes, and special effects had to be done on a very tight budget. Lugosi later recalled, "Everything that Tod Browning wanted to do was queried [by the studio]. Couldn't it be done cheaper? Would it be just as effective if . . . ? That sort of thing. It was most dispiriting."[6]

Another interesting production note reveals how movies of the period anticipated the now-common practice of shooting sequels back-to-back. Universal shot a Spanish-language version of *Dracula* simultaneously with the English version, using the same sets. A different cast and crew was used, including director George Melford, Carlos Villarías as the Count, and Eduardo Arozamena as Van Helsing. Villarías is generally considered the weak link in this version, unable to match the intensity of Lugosi in the part.

The English-language version of the movie opened in New York in 1931. Browning disliked the final version, claiming that the studio had butchered the film he wanted to make. Nonetheless, it was an instant hit, with 50,000 tickets sold within 48 hours. Eager to be frightened, audiences all across the country soon formed long lines in front of theaters.

Newspaper reports claim that a number of viewers actually fainted while watching *Dracula*. Browning's biographers, David J. Skal and Elias Savada, point out that this

*Actor Béla Lugosi (pictured in this 1931 movie poster with actress Helen Chandler) created an enduring character in his portrayal of Count Dracula. His charming, seductive vampire was a far cry from the grotesque and disturbing Max Schreck character.*

phenomenon might have been connected to the deeply stressful times: America was two years into the devastating misery of the Great Depression. They comment, "Dracula was a uniquely frightening picture that found its audience during a uniquely frightening year."[7]

Whatever the reason, the movie's success brought Universal's shaky finances back to life. It also inspired a sequel. Never mind that Van Helsing had killed the Count; Dracula refused to die. In fact, Universal brought him back several times, including 1936's *Dracula's Daughter* (with Lugosi and

# A Taste of the Film's Energies

The first movie known to invoke the name of Dracula for its main character was a now-lost 1921 Hungarian film, *Drakula halála (The Death of Dracula)*. Only a few publicity stills are known to exist, but an article by an unnamed Hungarian journalist, published while the movie was being shot, provides one of the few remaining clues about it. In his piece, the writer describes one scene in particular:

> Drakula's wedding gives a taste of the film's energies. There is an immense hall, dressed in marble, with a very, very long and dark corridor in the middle. That is where Drakula lives his mysterious life. It is night. The flutter and shrieks of a multitude of beasts can be heard, and the door in the middle of the hall opens. Beautiful women parade through it, all dressed in dreamlike costumes, all of them being Drakula's wives. But now Drakula awaits his new woman, the most beautiful and desirable of all. She will be welcomed with a rain of flowers.

> . . . When the film is finished, this scene will constitute just a small section of a four-act film. On the screen, this scene will not last more than five minutes, whereas it takes a full day's work to produce. The viewer, sitting in the theatre, will have no idea what extraordinary talent was required from the director to rehearse, shoot, and edit the sequences one by one.

Quoted in Gary D. Rhodes, "*Drakula halála* (1921): The Cinema's First Dracula," *Horror Studies*, vol. 1, no. 1, 2010, p. 29.

Gloria Holden as his daughter) and 1943's *Son of Dracula* (with Lon Chaney Jr.—already famous among horror-movie fans for his role as the Wolf Man).

Other studios also got in on the action. One was MGM, which produced *Mark of the Vampire.* The film starred Lugosi, but—since the studio could not use the name Dracula—this time he was Count Mora.

## The Vampire Returns

These post-*Dracula* movies were part of a larger phenomenon: a huge wave of popularity for horror movies. It mattered little that most of them were terrible—they were hits nonetheless. However, one film, produced by Columbia Pictures, was more interesting than most. *The Return of the Vampire* brought the ancient themes of the immortal undead into modern times.

*The Return of the Vampire* was set in London, England, and released in 1944, while World War II raged. The movie reflects the nightly bombings by German forces that London was then suffering. An explosion uncovers the tomb of a vampire named Armand Tesla (although, as played by Lugosi again, he bears a curious resemblance to Dracula). Once Tesla comes alive again, he plots a terrible revenge on some old enemies.

The enthusiasm among audiences for horror movies continued well into the 1950s. Popular taste is fickle, however, and cinematic vampires fell out of fashion during this time—replaced, in large part, by movie monsters that emerged from the public's fascination with aliens (as in *The Day the Earth Stood Still*) and atomic-produced monsters (like *Godzilla*). Vampires remained more or less in their coffins until the late 1950s, when they made a dramatic comeback.

# Chapter 2

# The Vampire Evolves

The studio that almost single-handedly brought vampire movies back to life in the late 1950s was an English company called Hammer Films. Hammer was already famous for cranking out dozens of lurid horror and adventure movies. Its output ranged from classic tales of Frankenstein and the Mummy to originals like *Slave Girls* and *When Dinosaurs Ruled the Earth*.

When Hammer added Dracula to its roster, the studio followed its standard guidelines for making a good horror movie. This meant living color, usually with plenty of bloody reds, along with elaborate sets but relatively few special effects. They also followed the Hammer tradition of using scripts and actors that varied drastically in quality.

## Are Vampires Always Messy Eaters?

The first in Hammer's series, released in 1958, was simply called *Dracula*. (In the United States it was retitled *Horror of Dracula* to avoid confusion with the Lugosi version.) Director Terence Fisher and screenplay writer Jimmy Sangster used some elements of Stoker's novel and Universal's movie. (A few years later, in 1962, the copyright on the novel went into the public domain, which meant that studios no longer needed permission from the Stoker estate.)

The British film censorship board—a very strict agency—hated Sangster's first drafts of the story. One official wrote in an internal memo:

> The uncouth, uneducated, disgusting and vulgar style of Mr. Jimmy Sangster cannot quite obscure the remnants of a good horror story, though they do give one the gravest misgivings. . . . The curse of the thing is Technicolor blood: why need vampires be messier feeders than anyone else? Certainly strong cautions will be necessary on shots of blood. And of course, some of the stake-work is prohibitive.[8]

The board drew up a list of requirements before the movie could be made. The vampires could not be too revolting. Women needed to be decently dressed. The violence had to remain minimal. Hammer had to tone down the version it shot for British audiences, unlike the gorier Japanese and American versions, so English audiences missed such touches as Dracula's face disintegrating as he died.

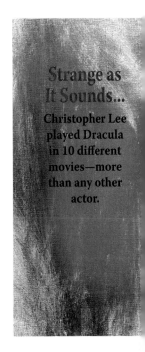

## The Horror of Dracula

The script that the censors finally accepted was set in 1885. Jonathan Harker travels to remote Germany, allegedly to become a librarian at Castle Dracula. In fact, he is a vampire hunter.

Harker has trouble from the start: He is bitten by a female vampire and starts to become a vampire himself. He succeeds in driving a stake through the woman's heart, but

Dracula escapes. Soon after, Harker's colleague Van Helsing arrives, sees that Harker has become a bloodsucker, and is forced to kill his friend with a stake through the heart.

Van Helsing returns to London and tells his story to Harker's friends Mina and Arthur, as well as Mina's sister Lucy (who was also Harker's fiancée). Meanwhile, Dracula secretly arrives in London and attacks Lucy and Mina, turning Lucy into a full-fledged vampire and Mina into a half-vampire—that is, only partially on her way to being undead. Van Helsing is forced to kill Lucy, but Dracula kidnaps Mina.

The Count returns home, with Van Helsing and Arthur in pursuit. They confront him in the castle and destroy him by tearing down curtains to let the sunshine in. As Dracula turns to dust, Mina is released from her half-vampiric state.

## The British Vampires Multiply

For the movie's London premiere, Hammer arranged a giant billboard outside the theater. Above the slogan "Every night he rises from his coffin bed silently to seek the warm flesh, the warm blood he needs to keep himself alive!"[9] was a picture of the actors playing Dracula and Mina. Mina had "real" blood flowing from her neck and dripping from her hair.

This stunt and other forms of publicity helped ensure the film's success despite the disgust of many members of the public and generally poor reviews. In fact, *Dracula* broke all attendance records for that theater. The controversy continued, however: When the movie played in the city of Birmingham, an advertising poster at the local blood bank had to be quickly removed after complaints.

As had Universal, Hammer produced many more *Dracula* movies after this success, as well as several vampire movies not featuring the Count. As might be expected, the *Dracula*

**Strange as It Sounds...**

In the first one and a half seasons of the TV series *Dark Shadows*, not one character uttered the word *vampire* in describing the mysterious, undead being known as Barnabas Collins, sequels had progressively less in common with the original story line. For one, they required elaborate opening scenes to explain how the bloodsucker managed to return after being killed over and over.

The Hammer films continued to be hits throughout the decade, but by 1970 audience interest was waning. In a bid to attract younger and wider audiences, the studio made the fifth in the series, *Scars of Dracula*, notably gorier. The strategy was not a success, however, and the movie bombed.

Hammer then tried another approach: moving Dracula out of the Victorian era. The first of these "contemporary" films was *Dracula AD 1972.* A disciple of Dracula schemes to bring his master back to life and convinces a group of freewheeling hippies to join him. But Dracula barely appears in the film, the hippies are played for laughs, and the movie flopped. After one more attempt to rejuvenate the series, Hammer returned to previous times with *The Legend of the 7 Golden Vampires*. When it bombed as well, Hammer finally killed off the series.

## The Stars

Hammer movies had small budgets, and saving money was always an issue. For example, *Dracula: Prince of Darkness* was filmed back-to-back with another production, *Rasputin: The Mad Monk*. They shared sets and cast, and watching them together shows how cleverly the recycled materials were used.

Despite the budget constraints, by all accounts working at Hammer was great fun. The lack of money fostered an atmosphere of improvisation, and the studio's small size encouraged a family-like atmosphere. Besides, Hammer made up for its low salaries by feeding the cast and crew well. Charles

**Strange as It Sounds...**

In an effort to capitalize on the success of the 1968 hit science fiction movie *Planet of the Apes*, some U.S. distributors changed the title of the Spanish vampire movie *La Noche del Terror Ciego (Night of Blind Terror)* to *Revenge from Planet Ape*.

Lloyd Pack, who played Dr. Seward in the first film, recalls those meals: "We could hardly move afterwards and work was very scarce in the afternoons."[10]

In all but two of Hammer's *Dracula* movies, the star was Christopher Lee. Lee's Dracula was very different from Lugosi's. In fact, Lee has remarked that he never looked at the Lugosi version when preparing his role, feeling that it would interfere with his interpretation.

At 6 feet 5 inches (1.98m) tall, Lee towers over nearly every actor he has ever appeared with. He also has a deep and commanding voice, but he did not need this to be convincing. In fact, in *Dracula: Prince of Darkness* he does not speak at all, using only his physical presence and an occasional hiss to instill fear. Director Terence Fisher comments, "His performance was superb in every respect. It is not a part that is dependent on dialogue. Its interpretation depends largely upon physical movement and facial expression, in other words, on a very real understanding of the art of mime."[11]

Costarring as Van Helsing is the lean-faced Peter Cushing. (They also had been paired in Hammer's *Frankenstein* movies, with Cushing as Dr. Frankenstein and Lee as the Monster.) Unlike previous movie vampire hunters, Cushing portrays Van Helsing as an athletic, physical fighter as well as an intellectual scientist. Although they were mortal enemies onscreen, off it Lee and Cushing were best friends. Together or separately, Lee and Cushing (who passed away in 1994) have appeared in hundreds of films. George Lucas, the man behind *Star Wars*, paid tribute to these iconic actors by casting Lee in several films as Count Dooku and Cushing as Grand Moff Tarkin in the original *Star Wars*. More recently, Lee appears in the *Lord of the Rings* trilogy (as Saruman the White) and supplies the roars of the Jabberwocky in *Alice in Wonderland* (2010).

*OPPOSITE: Hammer Films helped bring about a resurgence of vampire movies in the 1950s, beginning with the 1958 film* Horror of Dracula. *The film's American version had more gore than the British version because of intervention by the British film censorship board.*

## International Bloodsuckers

Although Hammer dominated vampire movies during this period, other studios also tried their hands at the legend. Some of these films were for specialized audiences, such as an ultra-low-budget Turkish movie in which crucifixes were not used as weapons (Turkey was, and is, a largely Muslim nation), or the Tagalog-language *Mga manugang ni Drakula (Son of Dracula)* from the Philippines.

Spanish- and Italian-speaking audiences were especially enthusiastic, and most non-English vampire films of this period were in those languages. Many aficionados feel that Spanish director Amando de Ossorio created the best of these. Ossorio devised a story line around the Knights Templar, a real-life medieval order of monks who, in the director's imagining, sought eternal life by drinking human blood.

In the first of his films, *La Noche del Terror Ciego (Night of the Blind Terror)*, the warriors are killed for their evil deeds and return in the modern world as rotting corpses. The vampires are blind—when they were killed, crows pecked their eyes out—and must find their victims using sharp hearing.

Another Spanish director, Jesus (Jesse) Franco, also made several popular vampire movies, notably 1970's *El Conde Dracula (Count Dracula)*. This film stars none other than Christopher Lee—the only time the actor plays Dracula in a movie not made by Hammer. Lee agreed to the project because its screenplay was a fairly faithful adaptation of Stoker's original story. The film is also notable for the presence of an intense German performer, Klaus Kinski, as Renfield. A few years later, Kinski would take on the vampire role himself.

# The Hammer Studios Style

England's Hammer Studios produced a number of very popular *Dracula* movies in the 1960s and the 1970s, in addition to many other horror and adventure films. A taste of Hammer's trademark style—gaudy, over-the-top, slightly self-mocking—can be had in this excerpt from the opening voiceover for *The Brides of Dracula*:

> Transylvania, land of dark forests, dread mountains and black, unfathomed lakes, still the home of magic and devilry as the nineteenth century draws to its close. Count Dracula, monarch of all vampires, is dead. But his disciples live on, to spread the cult and corrupt the world.

The reality of everyday filmmaking at Hammer, however, was much more down-to-earth. The studio's small size and tight budgets led to a friendly atmosphere on the set. That feeling can be glimpsed in this passage from actress Barbara Shelley, the studio's "scream queen," as she describes having trouble with the fangs she needed to play a vampire in one scene:

> I had to walk into a big close-up and . . . say the line, "You don't need Charles." The fangs were a tremendous impediment and so it came out like, "Hew gon't gleed Kharlz," at which, of course, everybody just roared with laughter, and I had to go into my dressing room for about 20 minutes and practice very carefully speaking around the fangs.

Hammer Films, *The Brides of Dracula*. www.hammerfilms.com. Wayne Kinsey, *Hammer Films: The Bray Studio Years*. London: Reynolds & Hearn, 2002, p. 317.

## Vampires Invade the Small Screen

Starting in the late 1940s, horror movies—and movies in general—were facing a new threat: television. Curiously, even though television audiences grew rapidly in the 1950s, it was not until the mid-1960s that vampires infiltrated broadcasting to any degree. The most significant of these appearances was on *Dark Shadows*.

This much-loved series, which debuted in 1966, was essentially a soap opera with supernatural elements. *Dark Shadows* follows Victoria Winters, an orphan in search of clues to her past. Hired by the wealthy Collins family as a governess, she is soon entangled in the mysteries that surround the family and its spooky mansion.

The program had mediocre ratings for six months—until a vampire entered. This was Barnabas Collins, introduced as the family's cousin from England. Barnabas was not initially a major character, but fans loved him. Actor Jonathan Frid was deluged with mail, and almost overnight he became a huge celebrity. Taking advantage of this, *Dark Shadows* creator Dan Curtis made Barnabas its main focus.

## Obsessed Teenagers

Especially from today's perspective, the series seems amateurish and improvised. Because of their schedule, the producers had difficulty going back to repair mistakes. As a result, viewers can see actors flub their lines or make up dialogue; props fall apart without warning; and the occasional stagehand can be spotted in the background. However, fans would not have it any other way; the mistakes and improvisations were part of the show's appeal. A huge number of those fans were teenagers, who were typically coming home from school just as the show aired. This rabidly loyal audience was outraged when the series was canceled in 1971. Even after leaving the air, however, *Dark Shadows* refused to die, and its impact is still felt. Director Tim Burton, writer Stephen King, and actor Johnny Depp are just three of the many artists who were deeply influenced by *Dark Shadows*. Burton comments, "It had the weirdest vibe to it. I'm sort of intrigued about that vibe. . . . It's like any great fable or fairytale, it's got a power to it."[12] Since, together or separately, these three have helped create some of the most successful movies ever, clearly Barnabas Collins has left his mark on film history.

## Remaking a Classic

Several more vampire stories were produced in the 1970s. The most significant of these—one that is startlingly different from the lurid Hammer films or the campy *Dark Shadows*—set out to make vampires genuinely scary again.

This was a German movie, *Nosferatu the Vampyre* (also called *Nosferatu: Phantom der Nacht*). It was a brilliant remake of Murnau's pioneering film. Its director, Werner Herzog, often told interviewers that he considered the first *Nosferatu* to be the greatest movie ever made in Germany.

*Christopher Lee plays the central character in* Dracula AD 1972, *a Hammer Films movie in which a Dracula disciple schemes to bring his master back to life.*

Herzog's remake faithfully re-created many of the original's most famous scenes, sometimes shot for shot. At the same time, it deepened its explorations of the story's themes, and it restored details Murnau had been forced to drop because of copyright concerns. The result, *Los Angeles Times* critic Kevin Thomas notes, helped viewers understand the power of early films, which managed to convey feelings through images and without the use of sound. *Nosferatu*, Thomas writes, was "a tribute to the purity of vision of the silent cinema."[13]

Kinski, the intense actor who had played Renfield in *El Conde Dracula*, this time acts in the role of the vampire, complete with ratlike teeth, bald head, and strange, long fingernails. A gifted cast of actors support him, including Bruno Ganz as Jonathan Harker and Isabelle Adjani as Lucy Harker (a combination of the original characters of Lucy and Mina).

The volatile Kinski was famous for his temper, but the equally intense Herzog found a way to control the actor. Kinski's makeup took several grueling hours each day to apply, and the director only had to threaten him with an extra makeup session. He comments, "If Kinski would start a tantrum, it would be four hours of makeup again."[14]

## 11,000 Painted Rats

Two versions of *Nosferatu the Vampyre* were shot, in German and in English, since all of the main actors were bilingual. Filming took place mainly in Czechoslovakia and in Delft, an ancient city in the Netherlands.

The authorities in Delft were apparently not pleased to have the notoriously moody director, his temperamental star, and their crew in town. Among other things, they refused to give Herzog permission to release 11,000 rats in

# *Dark Shadows* Goes to the Movies

In the 1960s the massive popularity of the television vampire soap opera *Dark Shadows* sparked the production of two feature films. The first, *House of Dark Shadows*, was more adult and frank in content than the television show, with what *Dark Shadows* expert Stuart Manning calls "a messy, corpse-laden ending." Although it was inexpensively shot, using the same cast and sets as the TV series, it was one of the most profitable movies of 1970 for its studio, MGM.

A second film, *Night of Dark Shadows*, was planned in 1971 after the series had been canceled. The star, Jonathan Frid, who had played vampire Barnabas Collins for years, was tired of the role and wary of being typecast. A new story line was therefore devised, focusing on other characters. This film was also a financial success. Manning writes:

> Without the headaches of producing the television series concurrently, the production crew [was] able to achieve a far more polished product than the previous year. Spiritualist Hans Holzer was employed as an advisor to the production, to give the production some authenticity, though . . . his actual contribution to the finished product proved minimal.

Stuart Manning, "Dark Shadows at the Movies," *Dark Shadows Journal*. www.collinwood.net.

the streets for one scene, and he was forced to relocate elsewhere for that shot. Furthermore, Herzog insisted on using gray rats. When his producers could find only white lab rats in that quantity, his crew painted them gray.

This attention to such details fills *Nosferatu the Vampyre* with startling visuals that do not need to rely on special effects. One, for example, shows the ship carrying Dracula's coffin as it slowly, silently noses its way, captainless, through the canals of Delft. As a result, critic David Denby notes, it resembles "not a conventional horror film (there are no shocks) but an anguished poem of death."[15]

Not every critic liked the film, however. Vincent Canby of the *New York Times* writes:

> Mr. Herzog has done what he set out to do, but when you come right down to it, one wonders if it's worth the trouble. Dracula, after all, is not Hamlet or Othello or Macbeth. He's not some profoundly complex character who speaks to us in more voices than most of us care to hear. Dracula is Santa Claus turned mean. He's a fairy-tale character. Though he represents something vestigially [slightly] scary, he's not endlessly interesting.[16]

Herzog's movie was dreamy and stark, and the Hammer films were gaudy and fun. These were, however, by no means the only kinds of vampire movies being produced. As the 1980s rolled in, new elements began to dominate, combining humor and romance with the thrills and chills—and also taking advantage of increasingly sophisticated special effects. In short: The era of blockbuster films was beginning.

# Chapter 3

# Blockbusters and Other Twists on an Immortal Tale

The decade of the 1980s launched the current era of vampire movies when it introduced a series of blockbuster films. Blockbusters are crowd-pleasing movies that feature lavish special effects, sky-high budgets, big thrills, and superstar actors and directors. Blockbusters began dominating not just vampire films but Hollywood movies in general, thanks to the wild successes in the 1970s of movies like *Jaws*, *E.T.*, and the *Indiana Jones* and *Star Wars* films.

In succeeding decades, vampire movies have continued to evolve. For example, in the 1990s a number of films emerged that saw the immortal dead in a new light: as sensitive, romantic, and complex characters that brought out the sympathy of audiences. More recently, the trend has shifted again. In the most popular vampire movies now, they have become still more humanlike, more sensitive, and all-around more attractive than ever before.

Not everyone appreciates the changes vampire movies have gone through over the years. These critics feel that the earlier vampire movies were the most genuinely frightening; they also dislike the more recent emphasis on sensitive vampires who value coexistence more than a blood meal. Grady Hendrix, writing in *Slate* magazine in 2009, laments that vampires are becoming less scary. He comments:

> You'll see vampires who manage nightclubs, build computer databases, work as private investigators, go to prep school . . . but the one thing you won't see them do is suck the blood of humans. No, bloodsucking is so yesterday . . . . Today's vampire is a good listener. He cares about our love lives and our problems, which is strange because we're supposed to be his food.[17]

However, other critics argue that the blockbuster trend helped bring vampires up to date, morphing stale, corny monsters into something that modern audiences could understand and enjoy. Like them or hate them, blockbusters went a long way toward keeping the immortal undead alive.

The blockbuster era for vampires arguably began with a TV miniseries, *Salem's Lot*, in 1979. Based on a Stephen King novel, it starred actors David Soul and James Mason and was directed by Tobe Hooper (who also directed, among other horror films, *The Texas Chainsaw Massacre*).

## Vampire Humor and Action

In this story, novelist Ben Mears returns to his hometown of Salem's Lot. He wants to rent an old mansion, but a man named Straker has already rented it. Straker opens an antique store with his business partner Kurt Barlow. As audiences learn, Barlow is an ancient vampire, and Straker is his servant. Soon, people start disappearing, then they return as vampires. Mears, his girlfriend, and others set out to destroy them. They appear to succeed—but only at first.

*Salem's Lot* was a huge hit on American TV and received three Emmy nominations. It also played in movie theaters in Europe. This success helped trigger other vampire projects in Hollywood. Among them was a 1985 horror/comedy film, *Fright Night*, about a boy named Charley Brewster (William Ragsdale) who discovers that his new neighbor (Chris Sarandon) is a vampire. Adults do not believe the kid, of course—except for the host of a local horror-film show, with whom Charlie is able to stop the vampire.

Two years later, Hollywood offered another successful movie combining comedy and bloodsucking thrills. *The Lost Boys* is about two brothers, Michael (Jason Patric) and Sam (Corey Haim), who live on the California coast. Strange things are happening, and their town is being terrorized by gang activity and disappearances.

The disruption is coming from a band of vampires, the Lost Boys. Their leader David (Kiefer Sutherland) persuades Michael to join them, and the new recruit begins to become a vampire: He sleeps all day, is sensitive to sunlight, and creates no reflection in mirrors. Romance enters the scene when Michael is drawn to David's girlfriend, Star (Jami Gertz). Meanwhile, Sam's brother meets two vampire hunters, who say that Michael (now a half-vampire) will return to normal if David is killed with a wooden stake. But a twist is in store. The key to ending the terror turns out not to be David but another vampire whose identity is eventually revealed to all.

# Casting Edward

When Catherine Hardwicke, the director of *Twilight*, was casting the movie, she chose Robert Pattinson for the all-important role of Edward Cullen. In this passage, Stephenie Meyer, the author of the *Twilight* books, comments on one of Hardwicke's choices:

> Of course, I have a mental picture and, unfortunately, people can't climb into my head and pull those out to use them. But, I'm actually amazed, particularly with Rob because Edward was a really hard one to cast. It was tough. I didn't really know if there was anyone who could do it. I knew it was going to be a version of Edward, but I didn't know what it was going to be.
>
> When they told me Rob was probably the one, I looked him up and thought, "Yeah, he can do a version of Edward. He's definitely got that vampire thing going on." And then, when I was on set and I got to watch him go from being Rob to shifting into being Edward, and he actually looked like the Edward in my head, it was a really bizarre experience. It was kind of surreal and almost a little scary. He really had it nailed. So, that was an amazing thing for me. That was very positive.

Quoted in Christina Radish, "*Twilight*'s Author and Director Talk About Bringing the Film to Life," *MediaBlvd Magazine*, September 17, 2008. www.mediablvd.com.

## Bram Stoker's Dracula

Some major vampire movies of the 1980s, such as *Fright Night* and *The Lost Boys*, appealed mainly to teen audiences by highlighting humor and action. In the next decade, however, another trend emerged, in which stories relied more on emotion and character. One was *Bram Stoker's Dracula*. Released in 1992, it was created by Francis Ford Coppola, the gifted director of the *Godfather* movies. His stars were Gary Oldman (Dracula), Winona Ryder (Mina Harker), Anthony Hopkins (Van Helsing), Keanu Reeves (Jonathan Harker), and Sadie Frost (Lucy Westenra).

Coppola's film stressed the romantic and tragic nature of Stoker's novel as well as the horror. (In fact, advertisements for the movie used the tagline "Love Never Dies.") In this imagining, Dracula makes Mina the target of his obsession, but she is just as fully fixated on him. The movie's visuals back this up: The strongest images of the Count are romantic and attractive, not ugly or horrifying.

The screenplay by James V. Hart is faithful to Stoker's story in many ways. For instance, Dracula changes shape and becomes younger when he feeds on blood. However, the filmmakers also altered the Count's character to make him richer and more sympathetic. For example, the movie starts with a prologue set in the fifteenth century. After his beloved wife kills herself, Dracula denounces God and swears revenge. This gives the audience an understanding of the Count's tragic past. When Dracula travels to England, the young and attractive aristocrat seduces Lucy and makes her a vampire. At the same time, he is obsessed with Mina—she looks like his long-dead wife. Mina, meanwhile, is helplessly attracted to him.

The concluding section—in a break with the novel—finds Dracula escaping to Transylvania, with Harker, Mina, and

Van Helsing in pursuit. They wound Dracula, but Mina rushes to his defense. The two flee to the chapel where he once had renounced God, and the dying vampire reverts to his fiendish form. Wanting only peace, he asks for death. When Mina tearfully gives this to him, she becomes human again.

## Restoring "The Creature's Nobility"

Coppola's version of *Dracula* was widely praised for its lush visual design and startling images. These effects were all done with traditional moviemaking techniques. The director avoided computer-generated effects, feeling that they would detract from the emotions of the movie.

Instead, he created low-tech but striking visuals. For example, in one scene Harker is shaving. As we watch from behind, Dracula approaches and places a hand on Harker's shoulder. The audience sees the vampire's hand but, in keeping with the Dracula legend, not its reflection in the mirror. This was achieved with a technique that has been used since the earliest days of the movies: The actor with his back to the camera is a double, not Keanu Reeves. The "mirror" is really a hole in the wall, with Reeves standing on the other side and facing the camera. Dracula is invisible in the mirror because there is no mirror.

The movie did well with audiences, and it won three Oscars (all in technical categories). Not everyone liked the film, however. Some viewers felt Coppola sentimentalized the tale by making the vampire too human and sympathetic. Others objected to the wooden acting of Keanu Reeves (who had not been Coppola's choice—his producers had insisted because they felt Reeves would draw large groups of teenage girls). Some critics complained that it felt flat or forced. For example, Tom Hibbert, writing in England's most promi-

*Transylvania, the place most closely associated with the Dracula stories, is situated in a mountainous, tree-covered region of Romania (pictured). At the end of Francis Ford Coppola's film, Dracula seeks refuge in Transylvania.*

nent film magazine, *Empire*, comments, "He [Coppola] fails to make his Dracula laughably lovable . . . and he fails to make it in any way frightening; he simply manages to make it terribly, terribly dull—an achievement in itself. . . . [The movie is] all style, no content. . . . Has a film ever promised so much yet delivered so little?"[18]

On the whole, however, critics generally liked Coppola's take on Dracula. Representative of them was *Time* magazine's critic Richard Corliss, who noted that the director had restored dignity and depth to what was often a stale figure of fun. Corliss writes, "Coppola brings the old spook story alive. . . . Everyone knows that Dracula has a heart; Coppola knows that it is more than an organ to drive a stake into. To the director, the count is a restless spirit who has been condemned for too many years to interment in cruddy movies. This luscious film restores the creature's nobility and gives him peace."[19]

## Interview with the Vampire

Soon after the release of Coppola's film came another big production. *Interview with the Vampire: The Vampire Chronicles*, released in 1993, was directed by another gifted filmmaker, Neil Jordan. Starring Tom Cruise and Brad Pitt, it was adapted from a best-selling novel by Anne Rice.

*Interview* maintains Coppola's strategy of stressing the sensitivity and sympathy of the immortal undead, despite the violence and sorrow they create. In this movie, some—but not all—vampires are tortured by their inability to age or die, and some hate having to kill.

As the movie opens, a reporter in San Francisco meets Louis (Pitt), who claims to be a vampire. Louis then relates his story, beginning in Louisiana in 1791. Louis is grieving the deaths of his wife and child when a stylish vampire named Lestat (Cruise) offers him the chance to be reborn—by becoming a vampire. Louis does so and sorrowfully travels through the centuries with Lestat—who proves to be vicious and self-centered—and their young vampire "niece" Claudia (Kirsten Dunst).

The shooting of the movie was done under a cloak of secrecy. Cruise insisted that he needed a private set because he wanted the vampire's makeup effects to remain a secret until the film was released. (He spent three and a half hours every day in the makeup chair.) Because of his concerns, tunnels were built to hide the actors as they traveled to and from the set.

*Interview with the Vampire* received mixed reviews and was nominated for two minor-category Oscars (but did not win either). The movie was only a moderate success at the box office; its violent images, decadent atmosphere, and baffling sexuality offended many viewers. One was Oprah Winfrey, who left the premiere before the end because she hated its cruelty. Others simply found the film pretentious, especially the odd accents that Cruise and Pitt used.

## Blade

In contrast to lavishly romantic movies like *Interview*, another trend in vampire movies began emerging in the 1990s. In some ways this trend was simply a continuation of the high-action films of the previous decade—with one difference. These films were based on characters from comic books and video games. Unsurprisingly, these films emphasized stylish imagery and fast action over character or plot.

One of the most successful of these was *Blade*, based on a superhero who originally appeared in a comic book called *The Tomb of Dracula*. Blade is a superpowerful half-vampire —a "daywalker" capable of withstanding sunlight. He is bent on revenge against vampires because his mother, bitten while pregnant, died while giving birth to him.

Released in 1998, *Blade* stars Wesley Snipes, rarely seen in the movie without his sword, long black leather coat, and dark sunglasses. (Others considered for the role include LL Cool J and Laurence Fishburne, who went on to star in the *Matrix* films.) Visually stylish, the movie used strange camera angles, unusual costumes and sets, and fast-paced editing, reflecting the film industry's increasing interest in swift storytelling.

Reaction to *Blade* and its two sequels was mixed. At the

# Vampires
# in Sweden

Vampire movies have evolved and changed over the last decades, emphasizing at various points powerful action, special effects, romance, graphic gore, and other characteristics. In some recent films, however, these traits have been put aside in favor of an emphasis on developing relationships between the main characters. A good example of this is a Swedish movie, *Låt den rätte komma in* (*Let the Right One In*), that was released in 2008.

In this movie, Oskar, a shy 12-year-old, develops a friendship with Eli, a vampire child in modern-day suburban Stockholm. They gradually become friends, and the young vampire encourages Oskar to stand up for himself against bullies. Their relationship deepens, and when Oskar cuts himself to form a blood bond with his friend, Eli cannot resist drinking Oskar's blood. Meanwhile, their close friendship is threatened by Eli's older companion, who kills for the younger creature and is jealous of their bond.

*Let the Right One In* was a surprise hit and won several international awards. It was so successful, in fact, that a remake in English, *Let Me In*, has also been produced.

box office, they were international smash hits. Their runaway financial success inspired the production of similar (and often also hit) movies based on comic book figures such as the X-Men, Spider-Man, Daredevil, and Iron Man. On the other hand, some people disliked *Blade*'s reversion to the violence of the some of the previous movies, such as *Interview with the Vampire*, as well as the gore in even earlier films, notably the Hammer productions.

## Inspiring More Fast Action

More recently, two other examples of vampire movies have extended the influence of *Blade* and other hyperactive, video-game-like films. Both star British actress Kate Beckinsale. In 2004's *Van Helsing,* she is a vengeful woman whose family was wiped out almost completely by Dracula. It co-stars Hugh Jackman as Gabriel Van Helsing, a vigilante monster hunter who is assigned to kill Dracula. (The name Van Helsing, of course, is a reference to the original vampire hunter in Stoker's book and many later versions of the famous tale.)

Beckinsale also stars in the *Underworld* saga, in which sophisticated vampires and thuggish, werewolf-like Lycans have been battling in secret for centuries. Beckinsale is Selene, a leather-clad vampire who discovers a Lycan plot that could prove fatal for her entire race—but who must make hard choices after falling for a human who is key to ending the war.

Although the *Underworld* films were generally panned by critics as shallow, they were also praised by some for their stylish look and carefully developed "back story" explaining the complex relationships among the various creatures. And they have been hugely popular; as of spring 2010, a fourth movie is in the works.

## The *Twilight* Juggernaut

Each of these movies was a major milestone in the history of vampire films, but the biggest milestone was yet to come: a series of runaway hits that powerfully combine horror, fantasy, and romance. The result is a cinematic vampire story with the widest audience in history.

As its millions of rabid fans know, this is the *Twilight* saga. Based on best-selling novels by Stephenie Meyer, the movies focus on a human teenager, Bella Swan (Kristen Stewart), who moves in with her father in Forks, a small town near the dark rain forests of Washington. Bella meets Edward Cullen (Robert Pattinson), who is 108 years old but looks like a teenager. Edward has mysterious powers and is part of a family of vampires who avoid human blood, preferring instead to hunt deer. A rival for Bella's affections, Jacob, provides the third part of a romantic triangle.

Bella (who has an unexplainable immunity to vampire powers) is confused at first because Edward seems to like her but also avoids her. He is indeed powerfully attracted to Bella but fears that he might succumb to his desire for human blood when near her. Nonetheless, their relationship continues to deepen, and he devotes himself to protecting her from a group of evil vampires.

## Making a Movie from a Book

Some fanatical followers of Meyer's novels were skeptical that a movie could match them. Before the 2008 release of the first film, *Twilight*, Internet chat rooms were abuzz with speculation. How close would the story in the movie adhere to the story told in the books? Would the actors fit the characters as described in the books?

Any film adaptation is going to be different from its source material, but the makers of *Twilight* knew they had to be extra careful to stay close to the spirit of the books. Producer Greg Mooradian comments, "It's very important to distinguish that we're making a separate piece of art that obviously is going to remain very, very faithful to the book."[20] Screenwriter Melissa Rosenberg adds, "Adapting a book is not simply taking the book and putting it in screenplay format. You would have the longest dull movie in the world."[21]

To keep *Twilight* from being "the longest dull movie in the world," some scenes were cut or altered. Other changes include merging some minor characters and introducing the evil vampires earlier to increase dramatic tension. The general consensus among fans seems to be that the moviemakers did a good job.

In part, Rosenberg notes, this is because Meyer was closely involved in the making of the movie, offering ideas for the screenplay and casting choices. The screenwriter praises Meyer's willingness to compromise and states, "She is incredibly collaborative, fluid and not precious about her work."[22]

## "Unabashedly a Romance"

When the first movie was released some critics were disdainful. Others, however, felt that it succeeded artistically because it was faithful to the book and also because it took the emotions of young adults seriously. One of these was Kenneth Turan, writing in the *Los Angeles Times*, who commented, "*Twilight* is unabashedly a romance. All the story's inherent silliness aside, it is intent on conveying the magic of meeting that one special person you've been waiting for."[23]

To no one's surprise, the eagerly awaited film was a phenomenon. It racked up more than $7 million in ticket sales just from opening midnight showings, and a total of $35.7

### Strange as It Sounds...

Director Francis Ford Coppola decided that the laws of physics would be suspended in his version of *Dracula*, so shadows move on their own, rats run along ceilings, and liquid drips up instead of down.

million on its first full day. Again to no one's surprise, the movie's ending made it clear that sequels were in the offing; indeed, *New Moon* and *Eclipse* were released in 2009 and 2010, respectively. Furthermore, the DVD of *Twilight* sold more than 9 million copies in 2009, making it the top-selling title of the year, and the DVD of *New Moon* sold some 4 million units over the weekend of its release, putting it on track to surpass its predecessor.

## Failed Vamps and *True Blood*

With the runaway triumph of *Twilight*, producers in Hollywood have rushed to release other movies with vampire themes. So far, they have been less successful (for example, the forgettable *Cirque du Freak*). An exception to these flops, however, has been television's *True Blood*. Although not a film, it deserves mention if only because of its high quality.

The show is based on another best-selling series of books, Charlaine Harris's Southern Vampire Mystery series. In the fictional Louisiana town of Bon Temps, vampires and humans live in close proximity. The main character is a waitress with telepathic powers, Sookie Stackhouse (Anna Paquin), who is in love with vampire Bill Compton (Stephen Moyer). Thanks to its setting and story line, the series entertains and also addresses such thorny issues as prejudice, gay rights, and intolerance.

*True Blood* was created by Alan Ball, who found Harris's novels while browsing in a bookstore. The show's premiere benefited from a massive advertising campaign that included an alternate reality game, comic books, giveaways of DVDs of the first episode, and fake commercials for TruBlood, a fictional drink on the show. A real-life version of the drink is even available, as is a line of *True Blood* jewelry.

When you can live forever, what do you live for?

*Stephenie Meyer's popular Twilight series, featuring the vampire Edward Cullen and the human teenager Bella Swan, has captured the hearts of teens.* Twilight, *the first book in the series, was an instant success when it made its movie debut in 2008.*

There are many parallels between *Twilight* and *True Blood*, notably that Sookie and Bella are both strong-willed young women, and both are humans who nonetheless have a natural sympathy for the supernatural. Many fans of both find *True Blood* more interesting as art. Stephanie Wichmann, an expert on vampire literature and films, comments, "I think looking at *Twilight* and *True Blood* side by side is really interesting, [although] *TB* is so much more sophisticated in terms of content and subtlety, lively character development, not to mention all of the links between gay rights and vampire rights."[24]

*True Blood, Twilight,* and other variations—both new and old—on the basic vampire story have each contributed their own twists to the immortal tale. The history of vampire cinema thus encompasses a wide variety of styles and storytelling. However, some common themes run throughout many—perhaps most—movies about the immortal dead. There are some surprising differences as well.

# Chapter 4

# The Building Blocks of Vampire Flicks

**A**ll through the history of vampire cinema, certain elements and themes recur. Some have remained more or less intact over time and across the many kinds of movies about the creatures. In other words, they arise from the dead again and again.

On the other hand, moviemakers the world over, and across the decades, have not hesitated to play around with the fundamentals of silver-screen bloodsucker traditions, inventing new twists on an old story. Whether movies remain true to the classic building blocks, are similar to them in some respects, or venture off into completely new territory, only rarely are they boring.

## Stakes, Decapitation, and Sunlight

Borrowing heavily from the characteristics of the ancient vampire legends is, of course, the tried and true route for filmmakers. In the mind of the public, these characteristics include the vampires' need for blood (human if possible) to stay immortal. Garlic, holy water, and/or crosses harm them. Sunlight tends to weaken or kill them.

Furthermore, they do not cast reflections in a mirror. They cannot enter a house unless invited, and they are afraid of running water. And, of course, the only sure way to kill them is by plunging wooden stakes into their hearts and/or decapitating them.

Within this basic framework, however, moviemakers have devised all kinds of variations. The method of killing, for instance, is by no means the same, even within Stoker's *Dracula*. The novel mentions several times that a wooden stake and decapitation are preferred. In the end, however, the Count himself is killed with two knives, one to the throat and one to the heart. Or take *Blade*, in which the title character relies, in large part, on his sword. The heroine of both the movie and television series *Buffy the Vampire Slayer*, meanwhile, uses a variety of superpowers that her mystical guardians, the Watchers, have given her.

The effect of sunlight is equally varied. In the Stoker novel and Coppola's filmed version, sunlight does not kill the Count, although it does weaken his powers. (The Murnau version of *Nosferatu* is the first instance in which a vampire will die if exposed to sunlight. This is the method that "Ellen," as the Mina character is called in the movie, uses to destroy the bloodsucking creature.)

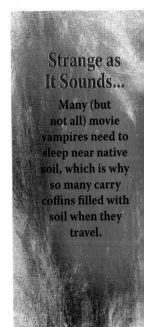

**Strange as It Sounds...**
Many (but not all) movie vampires need to sleep near native soil, which is why so many carry coffins filled with soil when they travel.

## From Claustrophobic to Elegant

The environments that Dracula moves in also change from film to film. Lugosi's castle is dark, dirty, and claustrophobic. The Hammer films, however, supply it with expensive furniture, freshly painted rooms, and lavish candelabras. Literature scholar Nina Auerbach comments:

*The tools of the vampire hunting trade vary from movie to movie. In* Blade, *released in 1998, the vampire hunter's tool of choice is a sword but he uses other weapons in later movies as can be seen in this scene from* Blade II, *released in 2002.*

Béla Lugosi made his first entrance in a crypt furnished with rats, coffins, cobwebs, and other inhospitable props. His hand creeps out of his battered coffin, but we never see his body move. . . .

By contrast, Christopher Lee's coffin, on which DRACULA is elegantly carved on a gleaming surface, is, like his castle, immaculate. The credits roll as we admire his taste and care in maintaining a coffin so handsome. . . .

Lee's décor announces his allegiance to a sleek future, not a dusty past; his Castle Dracula is a streamlined respite from the suffocating clutter of the . . . Victorian home.[25]

The tidiness of the Hammer sets, in fact, was the cause of a little concern when the films were being made. There was some discussion of scrapping them and starting fresh, but the studio lacked the funds. The wife of set designer Bernard Robinson was also doubtful. She recalls, "I said, 'Bernard, there were no cobwebs. Who did the cleaning?' I told Bernard that it didn't seem very logical. 'Of course it is,' he said. 'Magic!'"[26]

## The Way You Look Tonight

Just as the ways in which vampires can be killed have varied widely over the years, so do the ways in which they look and act. Consider just the most famous vampire of them all: Count Dracula. His appearance has been radically different from movie to movie.

Unlike Stoker's mysterious, handsome, and noble character, for instance, Count Orlok wears no tuxedo or cloak, nor does he bid fair maidens welcome. Instead, he preys upon innocent victims like a killer plague, satisfying his unquenchable thirst for human blood.

The two versions of *Nosferatu* also differ from Stoker's conception of how the vampire looks; they depict the Count as a horrible, ugly creature, bald and skeletal, with strange teeth and long fingernails. Far from being attractive or sexy, this concept of the bloodsucker is simply bizarre and terrifying. On the other hand, consider the characterizations created by Béla Lugosi, Christopher Lee, and Gary Oldman. For Lugosi, Lee, and Oldman (in most of his movie), Dracula is usually attractive, polite, aristocratic, and mesmerizing.

Coppola's movie is unusual in that it follows Stoker's depiction of Dracula as a shape-shifter (more, that is, than

# The Makeup of *Twilight*

Turning the actors in the *Twilight* movies into vampires presented a challenge to the production's makeup artists. They worked together with the film's special effects experts to create certain looks. For instance, for scenes in which the creatures transform, the special effects artists fit the actors with special teeth. Their eyes, meanwhile, were a combination of colored contact lenses and computerized imaging.

Robert Pattinson, who plays Edward, had to wear contact lenses—golden or black, depending on the scene—every day of filming. Makeup specialist Jeanne Van Phue chose to make Pattinson paler than the other vampires because she wanted each of them to have a distinctive look. She comments, "All of the vampires are pale, but I didn't want them to look ghoulish. I didn't want to contour, but I didn't want them to fade away, either."

Van Phue said that her biggest challenge on the set was the weather of the Pacific Northwest, where the films were shot. She says, "We were outside all the time, and it rained the entire time we were there. [Many] of the shots were exterior, and trying to fix make-up in the rain with wet face and wet brush was difficult." She experimented until she found the most useful product: "It [went] on flawlessly — no smudges or streaks. And I accidentally found out it was water resistant."

Makeup411.com, "Robert Pattinson as Edward Cullen in *Twilight*." http://makeup411.com.

simply turning into a bat). Oldman's Count is a young, handsome warrior in the opening scene set centuries ago, but when the action moves to the nineteenth century he is ancient and eerie, with a bizarre, towering hairdo. Later, he changes even more, appearing to Mina as young and handsome, while to the bolder Lucy he appears as a vicious, powerful beast.

And then there is the all-important question of fangs. It is a common belief that all vampires have them, but this is not always the case in the movies. The first known movie to actually show a vampire's fangs was a 1957 Mexican movie, *El Vampiro*. Since then, vampires with fangs have become commonplace—especially as the amount of explicit violence and gore has increased.

The way in which Dracula moves has also changed dramatically. Lugosi was fairly stationary, for instance (a characteristic that is also true for his movie as a whole). He moved relatively little as he acted. Christopher Lee, meanwhile, always moved with great deliberation, as befit his aristocratic interpretation of the role. In a 1979 version, the actor playing Dracula moves constantly. Auerbach comments, "The immobility of Béla Lugosi . . . dissolves in the incessant motion of Frank Langella, who is always touching, moving, dancing, climbing, or riding horses. . . . Langella's graceful hands replace Lugosi's transfixing eyes."[27]

## How the Other Vampires Look

Of course, Dracula is not the only cinematic vampire whose looks can be radically different from movie to movie. In the 1980s, for example, vampires tended to be seen at one of two extremes. Some, as in *Salem's Lot*, are raunchy, ugly, and repulsive—more akin to mindless zombies than to intelligent,

*In* Bram Stoker's Dracula, *a strange hairdo and decrepit features contribute to the ancient and eerie feel of Gary Oldman's vampire character. As in Stoker's book, Oldman's Dracula is a shape-shifter.*

manipulative, charming bloodsuckers. There is nothing re-
motely romantic about them. Others, such as the villainous
Tom Cruise and weary Brad Pitt in *Interview*, are shown
more in the romantic mold.

More recently, the trend is to show movie vampires as
young, stylish, and extremely good-looking. They also tend
to be sexy, sometimes in a dangerous way (like Catherine Deneuve in 1983's *The Hunger*), sometimes in a nonthreatening
way (the prime example being *Twilight*'s Robert Pattinson).

## Sympathy for the Vampire

The character of Edward, and the other vampires in the *Twilight* saga, are excellent examples of another important difference between today's movie vampires and those of past years. Many of the methods that vampire hunters of old used to ward off the creatures do not work with the new style of immortal undead. For example, holy water, sunlight, garlic, wooden stakes, and crosses have no effect on Edward. Furthermore, his habits are quite different, such as the fact that he does not sleep in a coffin. (Also, Edward never has to worry about not being seen in mirrors; his reflection appears just as those of humans do.)

Perhaps the most significant part of Edward's character, meanwhile, is the strength of his sympathetic, emotional, and even heroic nature. This is in marked contrast to previous vampires, although some have inspired pity for their tortured condition. Christopher Lee once commented about his famous character, "Dracula is not exactly pathetic, but there is a terrible dark sadness about him. He doesn't want to live, but he's got to, he doesn't want to go on existing as an undead, but he has no choice."[28]

For example, Stoker's creature and the vampires in both versions of *Nosferatu* are terrifying forces from some very deep, dark place—and animal-like in their single-minded quest for survival. So is Oldman's Dracula, for at least part of the movie. These vampires may evoke a degree of compassion for their tragic fates; nonetheless, they remain largely unsympathetic.

The characters in the 1977 Langella version, meanwhile, are turned on their heads: Dracula is dashing and valiant, Van Helsing and Seward are incompetent medical men, Harker is unpleasant, and Lucy and Mina are far less helpless and constricted than the women of earlier versions. Auerbach writes, "In this breathtaking if confusing movie, Stoker's good men are villains; Stoker's vampire is a hero; the women, victims no more, embrace vampirism with rapture as the sole available escape from patriarchy [dependence on a father figure]. W.D. Richter's screenplay never bothers to tell the familiar story; it retells it for its age."[29]

## Vampire Movies as Morality Tales

Everybody knows what vampire movies are all about, at least on one level: entertaining the audience and/or scaring it out of its socks. Plenty of blood and creepiness (and sometimes sexiness or romance) are thrown in for good measure. On a deeper level, though, vampire movies tell a richer and more complex tale.

As with so many other kinds of stories—modern ones as well as those that have been told for centuries—vampire movies are, at their cores, tales of the eternal struggle between good and evil. A vampire story, in this view, is a morality tale. The forces of good clash, usually successfully, with the powers of evil.

In some versions of the good-versus-evil theme, the two are clearly defined. In the immortal undead department, the classic example of this is *Dracula*, with the Count, of course, as evil's representative. In other vampire movies, the immortal dead are still the bad guys: *Salem's Lot*, *Nosferatu*, the Hammer films, *Blade*, and *The Lost Boys* are all examples. These vampires are just plain bad. Van Helsing and his counterpart vampire killers, meanwhile, are the chief characters standing for all that is positive. Van Helsing, a man who deeply trusts the powers of science and believes in the presence of supernatural creatures, is the only person capa-

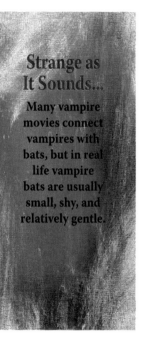

# I Am Legend

In 2007 a vampire movie called *I Am Legend* was released. It falls more into the category of suspenseful science fiction than horror. The film is based on a 1953 novel by a well-respected science fiction writer, Richard Matheson. In turn, according to Matheson, the novel was inspired by the Béla Lugosi version of *Dracula*. The author stated, "I thought if the world was full of vampires, it would be more frightening than just one. And I explained vampires in biological terms."

This movie (which stars Will Smith) was actually the third adaptation of Matheson's book. The first, in 1964, was a low-budget production, *The Last Man on Earth*, starring horror-film legend Vincent Price. Charlton Heston later took the lead role in a more elaborate 1971 version entitled *The Omega Man*.

In the Will Smith film, germ warfare has turned most of the planet's people into vampire-like creatures, but Robert Neville, Smith's character, is—for unknown reasons—immune. Neville thinks he may be the last human left in Manhattan, and perhaps on Earth. The film makes clear the plot's metaphoric connections to a real-life epidemic, that of AIDS. Neville, a scientist, is searching for a cure to a disease that does not kill but nonetheless destroys the health of its victims.

Lewis Beale, "A Variation on Vampire Lore That Won't Die," *New York Times*, January 14, 2007. www.nytimes.com.

*The central character of Stephenie Meyer's Twilight series is an attractive, sensitive, and caring vampire. Kristen Stewart (Bella) and Robert Pattinson (Edward) appear here in a scene from the 2009 movie* New Moon, *based on the second book in the series.*

ble of successfully fighting Dracula. Furthermore, brave Van Helsing provides the inspiration, cool thinking, and manly energy needed to spur others on in the face of terrible evil. As he muses in the Lugosi film, thinking about the elderly Seward and the relatively weak Harker, "I must be master here or I can do nothing."[30]

## Shades of Gray

Unlike earlier movies, which had simpler characters, many recent films have tried to create more complex vampires and vampire hunters. They strive to show that their characters can have elements of both evil and good at the same time. The division between the two is not always clearly defined.

Take, for instance, tortured Dracula in Coppola's film, grieving Louis in *Interview with the Vampire*, or sensitive Edward in *Twilight*. These vampires can be vicious—but they also hate having to prey on humans, and they are often not just attractive but genuinely likeable (these qualities are not the same, though they overlap). Furthermore, Langella's vampire is stylishly heroic but also a ruthless predator.

Beyond the vampire movie genre's symbolic figures of good and evil, the secondary characters tend to change considerably from film to film. In the various versions of *Dracula*, for instance, Mina Harker is portrayed quite differently. In some films she is demure and pure, willingly sacrificing herself to save others. In others, she is a passionate and strong-willed lover who becomes hopelessly enamored of the dark side of existence. Harker, too, changes from movie to movie: Sometimes he is brave and competent, sometimes weak and unpleasant.

## Religion, Death, and Resurrection

Another important aspect of many vampire movies is their subtext of religion. This topic is closely connected to the good-versus-evil theme that also runs through so many films. Specifically, Christianity and Christian symbols are often crucial elements.

Traditionally, crucifixes, rosaries, and holy water—all associated with the Christian religion—are among the best weapons to use in repelling the undead beings. Connections between vampires and the devil are often made explicit. And, in Coppola's vision of Dracula, the Count becomes a vampire after he renounces God. The implication is clear: Enlisting the aid of a higher power is a crucial part of fighting evil.

Another example of the close link between religion and the cinematic immortal undead is John Carpenter's *Vampires*. In this 1998 film a team of vampire hunters, sponsored by the Catholic Church, sets out to prevent a centuries-old cross from falling into the hands of a powerful vampire because it has the potential to make the creature immune to sunlight. The group's foul-mouthed, tough-as-nails leader, James Crow (James Woods)—who had watched his parents die at the hands of vampires—has the same initials as Jesus Christ. And the team stays at a desert motel called the Sun God.

Another fundamental theme of Christian theology that is also integral to vampire movies is the concept of resurrection—that is, of dying and returning to life. This is, of course, what happens to vampires. They do not die like mortals but are "born again" as the undead, hovering between life and death and condemned to wander forever—a concept similar to the Christian idea of purgatory, the temporary state in which souls are made ready for heaven. For vampires, however, this state is not temporary; the certainty of rest in the grave, the shelter of eternal life in heaven, is closed to them.

Over the years vampire movies have consistently played with just such notions—that is, with ways of linking the creatures with religious themes. Vampire movies have also experimented with other basic ideas from the legends of old, such as the use of various weapons that can harm them or keep them away. This evolution has provided an abundance of new blood for the genre.

# Chapter 5

# Breaking the Mold

No one would ever accuse the vampire movie genre of being stuffy or stuck in a rut. The ancient legends of the immortal dead have inspired countless works of art and entertainment—including movies—that more or less stick to the basics. But the basic story also lends itself easily to imaginative extension, so that new variations continue to flutter like bats around the genre's still-beating heart. Over the years, these variations have taken wildly different forms, from comedy, martial arts, and romance to gay/lesbian themes, science fiction, and the just plain strange.

## Fun with Vampires

One of the most durable of these variations is the comic vampire. The concept of making jokes about a serious or scary subject is nothing new. In fact, it is an ancient storytelling technique, since poking fun at something terrifying often makes it less frightening. Nonetheless, the first vampire movies were usually meant to scare audiences, not make them laugh. (Of course, modern audiences may find them funny, but that was rarely the intent.)

By the middle of the twentieth century, however, audiences needed something new. Dracula was world famous, but he and his undead friends no longer seemed frightening. Instead, vampires were becoming figures of fun—and so the tradition of Dracula spoofs was born.

One of the earliest of these comedies was released in 1948: *Abbott and Costello Meet Frankenstein*. Despite its title, the movie also features two other familiar figures: Dracula and the Wolf Man. In it, the classic comedy team of Bud Abbott and Lou Costello play freight handlers who take care of the remains of Frankenstein's Monster and Dracula as they are being shipped to a horror museum.

After these two bumblers lose the cargo, Dracula tries to transplant the brain of one of them into the head of the Monster. It takes an expert—the Wolf Man—to save the day. This movie is the only one in which Béla Lugosi plays Dracula again (although he did play vampires in three non-Dracula films: *Mark of the Vampire*, *The Return of the Vampire*, and *Mother Riley Meets the Vampire*).

### "Pardon Me, but Your Teeth Are in My Neck"

Another vampire spoof has become a cult classic: *The Fearless Vampire Killers, or: Pardon Me, but Your Teeth Are in My Neck*. It was directed by a distinguished filmmaker, Roman Polanski, whose other films include the horror classic *Rosemary's Baby* and the crime drama *Chinatown*, both considered among the best of their respective genres.

Polanski's comedy tells the over-the-top story of a bungling vampire hunter and his even dumber apprentice as they rescue a beautiful young woman from vampiric clutches. The high point of the movie is an elaborate ballroom scene during which vampires discover humans in their midst because, unlike the immortal undead, the humans are reflected in mirrors.

In later decades many more comedies saw the light of day,

including *Once Bitten*, best remembered now as one of Jim Carrey's first movies: He plays a teenager who becomes the target of a sexy vampire (Lauren Hutton). Nicolas Cage stars in *Vampire's Kiss* (1988) as a businessman who thinks he is becoming a vampire. This movie includes a scene in which the notoriously wild actor eats a real live cockroach (he later remarked, "Every muscle in my body didn't want to do it, but I did it anyway).[31]

Plenty of other spoofs have risen up as well, with varying degrees of quality. Among them: *Dracula: Dead and Loving It* (by Mel Brooks, the man behind another classic monster comedy, *Young Frankenstein*), Eddie Murphy in *Vampire in Brooklyn*, George Hamilton in *Love at First Bite*, and *Transylvania 6-5000* with Jeff Goldblum and Ed Begley Jr.

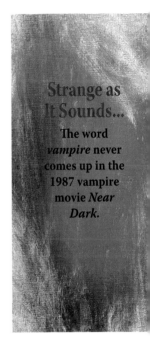

## Valley Girl Vamp

One of the most interesting offshoots of the classic vampire legend began as a disappointing movie but found enduring new life as a TV series. The movie, *Buffy the Vampire Slayer*, was a parody of vampire flicks. It was released in 1992, starring Kristy Swanson in the title role. However, it was not a success; *Buffy* was considered a failure artistically and at the box office. Its creator, Joss Whedon, later blamed the fact that the studio had changed it considerably from his initial idea, making it much lighter and sillier.

Far more successful was Whedon's darker and more imaginative adaptation of the idea for television. This show—also called *Buffy the Vampire Slayer*—ran from 1997 until 2003. In it, Buffy (played by Sarah Michelle Gellar) is a typical Southern California teenager—she is a cheerleader, and she loves to shop. As it happens, Buffy is also the latest in a dynasty of young women chosen to battle supernatural creatures.

*The television series* Buffy the Vampire Slayer *began life as a movie. Released in 1992, the movie did poorly but the television series earned a spot in* Time *magazine's "100 Best TV Shows of All Time." Pictured here is the show's star, Sarah Michelle Gellar.*

*Buffy* mixed dark comedy with a wide variety of other styles, from martial arts movies to musicals, and the high quality of its production and writing made it wildly popular—and deeply influential as well. For one thing, its success provided a taste of what was to come with the even more popular *Twilight* blockbusters. Millions of the fans of the TV series avidly followed every facet of "the Buffyverse," and they devoured huge quantities of Buffy products such as novels, comics, action figures, and video games.

Critics liked *Buffy* as well. *Time* magazine listed it as one of its "100 Best TV Shows of All Time." The series won numerous awards, including three Emmys. And Whedon, its writer-director, went on to create more highly original works, including *Serenity*, *Angel*, and *Firefly*.

## The Blood Countess

Buffy was not a vampire—she just fought them. However, many cinematic children of the night were also female. The Brides of Dracula and Claudia (the young vampire in *Interview with the Vampire*) are only a few examples. Another, one that many movie buffs consider the best, is the title character of Hammer's *Countess Dracula*, starring the veteran horror-film actress Ingrid Pitt.

*Countess Dracula* was inspired by a real person, Elizabeth Báthory. Born in 1560, Báthory was a wealthy Transylvania aristocrat—and a serial murderer known as the Blood Countess. According to legend, she tortured and killed (or had killed) hundreds of virgin girls. This was so that she could drink and bathe in their blood—the countess believed that it would keep her young. When her atrocities were discovered in 1610 a trial was held; several of her servants were beheaded, but the countess was imprisoned in her castle until her death in 1614.

Báthory probably inspired the classic horror novel *Carmilla*, written by Joseph Sheridan Le Fanu decades before Stoker wrote *Dracula*. In turn, *Carmilla* inspired a 1971 Belgian movie about an aristocratic female vampire, *Daughters of Darkness*. The Carmilla character has also inspired many other films, including *Vampyr*, *The Blood of Roses*, and a trio of Hammer movies with suitably lurid titles: *The Vampire Lovers*, *Lust for a Vampire*, and *Twins of Evil*.

Themes of lesbianism or bisexuality run through many vampire films as well. The most famous of these is *The Hunger*. It chronicles a bizarre love triangle between a doctor, Sarah (Susan Sarandon), and a vampire couple, Miriam and John (Catherine Deneuve and David Bowie). Miriam and John have been married for centuries and live in an elegant Manhattan townhouse.

Miriam does not age, but her companions (including John) become corpse-like and half-dead after about a century. In an effort to prevent this, John visits Sarah, who specializes in aging disorders. However, she cannot save him, he ages quickly, and Miriam puts him in a coffin alongside her other undead lovers.

Miriam then seduces and vampirizes Sarah. Sarah, in turn, kills her boyfriend and then herself. This sacrifice reverses Miriam's powers, and her former lovers rise up to kill her.

## Rockin' Vampires

There are countless more vampire movie variations. Consider, for example, the gloriously silly *Son of Dracula*, a rock musical starring singer Harry Nilsson (as the half-vampire Count Downe, who falls in love with a human) and ex-Beatle Ringo Starr (as his magician mentor). It flopped at the box office and got terrible reviews; according to some reports, Starr owns a copy but cannot bring himself to watch it.

Another musical vampire story was *Queen of the Damned*. Based on a sequel to Anne Rice's novel about Lestat, the vampire here is resurrected as a rock star. His music awakens another creature, Queen Akasha. The movie stars Stuart Townsend and Aaliyah, an up-and-coming singer who was

# Mr. Vampire

China has a long and varied tradition of ghost and vampire stories, and many films about them have been produced there. Some are comedies, such as the *Geungsi Sinsang* series of comedy/action/horror/romance films from Hong Kong. The first, released in 1985 in English under the title *Mr. Vampire*, was so successful that it spawned many sequels, some under the auspices of the first movie's writer-director Ricky Lau.

In the first film in the series, a priest is hired to rebury the corpse of a rich man named Yam. This is happening because a fortune teller told the dead man's son that it will bring good luck. When the priest and his assistants look at it, the corpse is still almost intact and looks alive. In fact, it rises up and becomes what the movie calls a "hopping vampire." (These vampires are so named because they can "hop" on their own feet back to their hometowns for proper burial according to Chinese custom.)

The vampire runs amok and kills many people (his son is the first to go). The priest and his foolish assistants try to destroy it. (One thing in their favor: They know that holding their breath will make them invisible to vampires.) The priest leads a group of friendly vampires against Yam. Yam knocks out all of the vampires, but the priest manages to drop a ceiling lantern on him, and the vampire is killed when he bursts into flames.

killed in an airplane crash only weeks after filming. It was poorly received, but its soundtrack was a hit.

A low-budget version of the vampire-music connection in the cinema is the darkly comic rock musical *Suck*, released in 2009 and written and directed by Canadian comic/actor Rob Stefaniuk. (*Suck* also features rockers Henry Rollins, Moby, Iggy Pop, and Alice Cooper in cameo roles.) Stefaniuk plays Joey, the leader of a struggling band called the Winners. The band enjoys sudden and unexpected fame when its lead singer, Jennifer (Jessica Paré), turns into a very seductive and sexy vampire.

A fourth example of rockin' vampire musicals is not exactly a feature film but deserves a mention. *I Kissed a Vampire*, a series first made available on iTunes, stars some of the cast members from *High School Musical*. It is advertised as the Web's only vampire rock musical.

## Deafula

No book about vampire movies would be complete without a look at the first feature film shot entirely in American Sign Language: *Deafula*. Cameraman and actor Peter Wechsberg wrote, directed, and starred in this ultra-low-budget, black-and-white 1975 curiosity. He plays Steve, a young deaf man who has a rare blood disease that requires a constant supply of fresh blood.

Steve's father has been giving blood for years to keep his son alive, but Steve still sometimes becomes a vampire. Two bumbling detectives set out to track him down; meanwhile, Steve encounters an old family friend who helps him realize that the original Dracula is his real father.

*Deafula* is astonishingly bizarre. For one thing, Steve's family friend has a servant with tin cans where his hands should be (which, in a world of deaf people, renders him mute). When it was released, *Deafula* featured a voice-over for hearing audiences. Obviously, though, this was not its target audience. The film's producer, Gary Holstrom, recalls that deaf viewers understood its purpose more than those who could hear:

> Audience reactions were fascinating. Where we could arrange it, extra bass speakers were placed near the screen. Pump up that bass and the deaf audience would scream with excitement. They could feel the suspense via vibration. . . . "[O]ne liners" brought the deaf to loud laughter. The hearing folks had a different reaction. It was quite an experience.[32]

Controversy has surrounded *Deafula* since its release—was it meant as a joke, or was it just really strange? It may be difficult for the public to decide for itself any time soon; the movie is not available commercially, and only a snippet can be seen online—although there are rumors of pirated copies.

## Vampires in Cowboy Hats

Another variation combines the immortal undead with Westerns. Perhaps the first of these was a low-budget oddity from 1966, *Billy the Kid vs. Dracula*. In it, Dracula slowly turns a beautiful young woman into a vampire; fortunately, her fiancé is Billy the Kid, who figures out what is going on.

Dracula is played by John Carradine, who also plays the vampire in other later Universal productions. He is considered to have a marked physical resemblance to Stoker's original description of the Count. However, Carradine does not even try to do a Romanian accent. As a result of this and other factors, like so many other low-budget movies, *Billy the Kid vs. Dracula* is funny—but not on purpose.

A less jokey and much darker combination of vampire and Western themes—with a little biker-movie action thrown in—is 1987's *Near Dark*, a cult hit cowritten and directed by Kathryn Bigelow (who in 2010 became the first female to win a Best Director Oscar). It concerns a man from a small Oklahoma town who is drawn into a wandering tribe of vampires.

Then there is *Sundown: The Vampire in Retreat*, a strange 1990 movie that combines a Western theme with vampires and comedy. All of America's vampires live in a small town, where they wear sunblock to protect themselves and survive by drinking a blood substitute—but a problem arises when the factory that produces it closes. Among the movie's actors are Maxwell Caulfield, David Carradine, and Bruce Campbell.

# Vampires Beneath Tokyo

Japan's centuries-old tradition of ghost and vampire legends has resulted in a huge number of horror movies about bloodsuckers being made there. One of the strangest is *Marebito* (*Spiritual Being*), an intense film written and directed by Takashi Shimizu and released in 2005. It is about a cameraman named Masuoka who is obsessed with videotaping odd events around Tokyo—especially those involving near-death or death. He is especially fascinated by footage of a person who committed suicide in a subway station. The cameraman finds himself wishing he could experience the same emotions as people who are about to die.

One day, Masuoka discovers a maze of tunnels beneath the city, the hiding place of the suicide victim and homeless people who are strange creatures that walk on all fours. He learns that the tunnels are also home to vampires called Deros. Exploring further, he finds a mute, beautiful girl imprisoned in a cavern. He takes her home, thinking she is human, but she is not—she is indeed a vampire. Masuoka uses his own blood to keep her alive, but he cannot supply enough. So he starts "borrowing" from others, beginning with his ex-wife.

Although the film has attained a small but loyal audience, it was in general not received well by moviegoers or critics. John Hartl of the *Seattle Times*, for instance, calls it a "gross-out ghost story. . . . The gloppy sound effects are so over-the-top, they invite laughter, and the bloodsucking scenes are allowed to become absurdly repetitious."

John Hartl, "*Marebito*: Keep an Eye Out for Gore," *Seattle Times*, February 3, 2006. http://seattletimes.nwsource.com.

And still another example of this mix-and-match approach to vampire/Western themes is *From Dusk till Dawn* (1996), which stars two moviemakers in unusual roles: Quentin Tarantino and George Clooney. As expected from Tarantino, the writer-director of *Pulp Fiction*, *Reservoir Dogs*, and *Kill Bill*, this movie is ultraviolent and cartoonish but with energy and wit to spare. Tarantino and Clooney play brothers and bank robbers on the run in Mexico.

At a desert bar they get into a fight, during which a beautiful vampire bites one of them. The surviving people trapped in the bar must band together to live through the night when the dead (including the robber) return as vampires.

*From Dusk till Dawn* aroused strong emotions from critics and audiences alike—they loved it or hated it, with most of them in the latter category. Janet Maslin of the *New York Times*, for instance, found it "promising" but asserts that its violence is too extreme to be taken seriously. She writes, "The latter part of *From Dusk Till Dawn* is so relentless that it's as if a spigot has been turned on and then broken. . . . The film loses its clever edge when its action heats up so gruesomely and exploitatively that there's no time for talk."[33]

## Strange as It Sounds...

Not all movie vampires must avoid sunlight; the vampires in *Twilight* and *Blade* are just a few of the undead characters who can walk in the daytime.

## Looking for Cures

Other vampire movies weave horror with medical or scientific themes. One example is Korean director Park Chanwook's *Thirst*, a disturbing film about a priest who volunteers to help develop a vaccine for a deadly virus. When the experiment goes wrong he nearly dies, then recovers with a transfusion. Unfortunately, he is accidentally given the blood of a vampire.

Park, one of South Korea's top directors, has stated that he was intrigued by the idea of combining, in one person, an evil vampire and a selfless priest. He comments, "Between these two identities, there is a huge ethical gap. . . . You have the moral height of being this noble priest, and the moral downfall to where you become a vampire."[34]

Another movie with a medical theme is 2010's *Daybreakers*. It stars Ethan Hawke and was written and directed by Michael Spierig and Peter Spierig. The movie is set in the near future, when a disease has turned most humans into vampires. They are multiplying, and without enough blood they turn wild and blindly attack the uninfected humans. As the human population nears extinction, survivors are captured and "farmed" for their blood. Hawke plays a vampire scientist working to find a synthetic substitute.

## Into the Future

As of early 2010 a number of new cinematic bloodsuckers are on the way. For instance, Sigourney Weaver is scheduled to play the queen of the vampires in the horror comedy *Vamps*, in which two "vampirettes" (Alicia Silverstone and Krysten Ritter) put their immortality at risk by falling in love with human boys.

Tim Burton, meanwhile, is set to produce a version of the best-selling novel *Abraham Lincoln, Vampire Hunter*, and he and Johnny Depp are reportedly working on an adaptation of *Dark Shadows*. Furthermore, movies mimicking the success of *Twilight* are in the works. All told, with a century of rich and varied history behind them, vampire movies seem to be in no danger of fading to black.

**Strange as It Sounds...**

In the 1978 movie *Martin*, the title character, who may or may not be a *real* vampire, uses a hypodermic needle instead of hypnotism to control his victims, and uses razors instead of fangs.

# Source Notes

## Introduction: Blood-Sucking Stars of the Silver Screen

1. Quoted in Wayne Kinsey, *Hammer Films: The Bray Studio Years*. London: Reynolds & Hearn, 2002, p. 101.

## Chapter 1: Dawn of the Movie Undead

2. Quoted in David J. Skal and Elias Savada, *Dark Carnival: The Secret World of Tod Browning, Hollywood's Master of the Macabre*. New York: Anchor, 1995, p. 137.
3. Gregory A. Waller, "Tod Browning's Dracula," in *Dracula: Bram Stoker*, ed. Nina Auerbach and David J. Skal. New York: Norton, 1997, p. 383.
4. Quoted in Imbd.com, "Memorable Quotes," *Dracula*. www.imdb.com.
5. Quoted in Skal and Savada, *Dark Carnival*, p. 153.
6. Quoted in Skal and Savada, *Dark Carnival*, p. 150.
7. Skal and Savada, *Dark Carnival*, p. 157.

## Chapter 2: The Vampire Evolves

8. Quoted in Kinsey, *Hammer Films*, p. 94.
9. Quoted in Kinsey, *Hammer Films*, p. 126.
10. Quoted in Kinsey, *Hammer Films*, p. 104.
11. Quoted in Kinsey, *Hammer Films*, p. 104.
12. Quoted in Matt McDaniel, "Johnny Depp and Tim Burton to Vamp It Up in 'Dark Shadows,'" Yahoo! Movies. http://movies.yahoo.com.

13. Kevin Thomas, "New 'Nosferatu' a Tribute to Murnau," *Los Angeles Times*, October 29, 1979.
14. Quoted in "Werner Herzog on *Nosferatu*." www.hatii.arts.gla.ac.uk.
15. David Denby, "In Praise of Older Women," *New York Magazine*, October 22, 1979. http://books.google.com.
16. Vincent Canby, "Nosferatu," *New York Times*, October 1, 1979. http://movies.nytimes.com.

## Chapter 3: Blockbusters and Other Twists on an Immortal Tale

17. Grady Hendrix, "Vampires Suck," *Slate*, July 28, 2009. www.slate.com.
18. Tom Hibbert, "Bram Stoker's Dracula," *Empire*. www.empireonline.com.
19. Richard Corliss, "A Vampire with Heart," *Time*, November 23, 1992. www.time.com.
20. Quoted in Larry Carroll, "'Twilight' Tuesday: How Faithful Will the Movie Be to the Book?" MTV Movies: News, June 17, 2008. www.mtv.com.
21. Quoted in Marian Liu, "Screenwriter Embraces, Adapts 'Twilight' Universe," *Seattle Times*, March 19, 2010.
22. Quoted in Liu, "Screenwriter Embraces, Adapts 'Twilight' Universe."
23. Kenneth Turan, "You Wanna Neck?" *Los Angeles Times*, November 21, 2008. http://articles.latimes.com.
24. Stephanie Wichmann, e-mail to author, April 18, 2010.

## Chapter 4: The Building Blocks of Vampire Flicks

25. Nina Auerbach, "Vampires in the Light," in *Dracula: Bram Stoker*, eds. Nina Auerbach and David J. Skal. New York: Norton, 1997, pp. 391–93.
26. Quoted in Kinsey, *Hammer Films*, p. 99.
27. Auerbach, "Vampires in the Light," p. 399.
28. Quoted in Kinsey, *Hammer Films*, p. 104.
29. Auerbach, "Vampires in the Light," p. 398.
30. Quoted in Nina Auerbach, *Our Vampires, Ourselves*. Chicago: University of Chicago Press, 1997, p. 78.

## Chapter 5: Breaking the Mold

31. Quoted in Erin Free, "Vampire's Kiss," Filmink (Australia), January 26, 2009. www.filmink.com.
32. Quoted in Mike White, "Deafula." *Cashiers du Cinemart*, no. 13. www.impossiblefunky.com.
33. Janet Maslin, "From Dusk till Dawn," *New York Times*, January 19, 1996. http://movies.nytimes.com.
34. Quoted in Joe Ituchi, "Director Park Chan-Wook Talks *Thirst*." Rotten Tomatoes Interviews, July 30, 2009. www.rottentomatoes.com.

# For Further Exploration

## Books

DK Publishing, *The Vampire Book*. New York: DK, 2009.

Joshua Gee, *Encyclopedia Horrifica*. New York: Scholastic, 2007.

Rosemary Ellen Guiley, *Vampires*. New York: Checkmark, 2008.

Kris Hirschmann, *Vampires in Literature*. San Diego, CA: ReferencePoint Press, 2010.

## Web Sites

**How Vampires Work** (http://science.howstuffworks.com/vampire.htm). An excellent primer, with some especially good information on very early vampire myths.

**Monstrous Vampires** (http://vampires.monstrous.com). This site has lots of information on Vlad the Impaler, vampire legends, and much more.

**A Short History of Vampire Movies** (www.mrmovietimes.com/movie-news/a-short-history-of-vampire-movies-part-i-the-1920s). A MovieTimes.com site with excellent details, especially on some of the more obscure films.

**StephenieMeyer.com** (www.stepheniemeyer.com/twilight.html). The official Web site of the writer behind the Twilight series phenomenon.

**Vampire Filmography** (www.wsu.edu/~delahoyd/vampirefilms.html). A professor of English at Washington State University maintains this page on his Web site. It lists a great many vampire movies.

# Index

Note: Boldface page numbers refer to illustrations.

## A

*Abbott and Costello Meet Frankenstein,* 64
Abraham Van Helsing *(Dracula),* 7, 17–18, 24, 27, 39–40, 58, 60
action trend, 36–37, 39, 43, 45
American Sign Language vampire movie, 71–72
Auerbach, Nina, 51–52

## B

Barnabas Collins *(Dark Shadows),* 24, 30
Báthory, Elizabeth, 67
bats, 58
Bella Swan *(Twilight),* 46
Ben Mears *(Salem's Lot),* 36–37
Bill Compton *(True Blood),* 48
*Billy the Kid vs. Dracula,* 72
bisexuality, 68
*Blade* and sequels, 43, 45, 51, **52**
Blaskó, Béla Ferenc Dezső. *See* Lugosi, Béla
blockbuster trend, 35–37
Blood Countess, 67
*Bram Stoker's Dracula,* 39–42, 47, 51
*Brides of Dracula, The,* 29
Browning, Tod, 15, 18
*Buffy the Vampire Slayer,* 51, 65–67, **66**
Burton, Tim, 31

## C

*Carmilla* (Le Fanu), 67–68
child vampires, 44
Christianity, 61–62
comedy trend, 63–67
*Conde Dracula, El (Count Dracula),* 28
Coppola, Francis Ford, 39–42, 47
*Countess Dracula,* 67

Cruise, Tom, 42, 43
Cushing, Peter, 27

## D

*Dark Shadows* (television series), 24, 30–31, 33
*Daybreakers,* 75
*Deafula,* 71–72
Dracula
    continuing popularity of, 7
    in Hammer Films series, 22–25, **26,** 27, 29, **31**
    in original *Dracula* (1931), 16–18
    in recent movies, 39–42, 53, 55, **56,** 57–58
    in Stoker novel, 5–7, 13, 51
*Dracula* (1931), 15–19, **19**
*Dracula* (1958), 22–25, **26**
*Dracula* (Stoker), 5–7, 13, 51
*Dracula AD 1972,* 25
*Dracula's Daughter,* 19, 21
*Drakula halála (The Death of Dracula),* 8–9, 20
Dreyer, Carl Theodor, 12

## E

early talkies, 12, 14–19, **19,** 21
Edward Cullen *(Twilight),* 35, 38, 46, 57

## F

*Fearless Vampire Killers, The,* 64
Fisher, Terence, 7, 22, 27
foreign-language vampire movies
    Chinese, 69
    German, 8, 9–12, **10, 14,** 16, 31–32, 34, 57
    Hungarian, 8–9, 20
    Japanese, 73
    Mexican, 55
    Spanish, 18, 25, 28

Swedish, 44
Tagalog, 28
Turkish, 28
Fort, Garrett, 15
Frid, Jonathan, 30, 33
*Fright Night*, 37
*From Dusk till Dawn*, 74
future releases, 7, 75

**G**
Galeen, Henrik, 9

**H**
Hammer Films, 22–25, **26**, 27–28, 29, **31**, 34, 53
Herzog, Werner, 31–32, 34
horror genre (non-vampire), 8, 21, 22
*Horror of Dracula. See Dracula* (1958)
*House of Dark Shadows*, 33
*Hunger, The*, 68

**I**
*I Am Legend*, 59
*I Kissed a Vampire*, 70
*Interview with the Vampire: The Vampire Chronicles*, 42–43, **70**

**J**
John Seward (*Dracula*), 6–7, 17–18
Jonathan Harker (*Dracula*), 5–7, 9, 17–18, 23–24, 39–40

**K**
key elements of vampire movies
basic/common, 50–51, 74
fright level, **10**, 12, 16, 35–36, 43, 45
gore level, 22–24, 27
portrayal of secondary characters, 57–58, 60–61
portrayal of vampires
bonds with non-vampires, 44

female, 45, 67–68
as heroes, 43, 44, 57–58
as villains, 12, 53, 57, 58
increasing complexity of, 57, 60, 61
physical appearance of, 13, 53–55
as romantic, 39, 46, 47, 56
as sympathetic, 35–36, 40, 42, 57
setting, 20, **41,** 52–53
weapons used by hunters, 51, **52**, 57, 61
Kinski, Klaus, 28, 32
Kurt Barlow (*Salem's Lot*), 36–37

**L**
Lajthay, Károly, 9
Langella, Frank, 55
Le Fanu, Joseph Sheridan, 14, 67–68
Lee, Christopher, 23, 27, 28, **31**, 53, 55
*Legend of the 7 Golden Vampires, The*, 25
legends, 4–5
lesbianism, 68
*Lost Boys, The*, 37
Lucy (*Dracula*), 5–6, 17–18, 24
Lugosi, Béla, 15–16, 17, **19**, 53, 55, 64

**M**
*Marebito (Spiritual Being)*, 73
*Mark of the Vampire*, 21
Matheson, Richard, 59
medical/scientific trend, 74–75
Meyer, Stephenie, 35, 38, 46, 47
Mina Murray Harker (*Dracula*), 5–7, 9, 17–18, 24, 39–40, 61
morality tales, 58, 60
*Mr. Vampire* series, 69
Murnau, F.W., 9, 11–12
mysteries, 48–49

**N**
*Nachte de Grauens (Night of Terror)*, 8
*Near Dark*, 72
*Night of Dark Shadows*, 33

*Noche del Terror Ciego (Night of the Blind Terror)*, 25, 28
*Nosferatu*, 9–12, **14**, 57
*Nosferatu the Vampyre*, 31–32, 34, 57

**O**
Oldman, Gary, 39, 57
*Once Bitten*, 65
Orlok (*Nosferatu*), 9–12
Ossorio, Amando de, 28

**P**
Pattinson, Robert, 35, 38, **49**, 54, **60**
Polanski, Roman, 64

**Q**
*Queen of the Damned*, 68, 70

**R**
Reeves, Keanu, 39, 40
religious themes, 61–62
Renfield (*Dracula*), 16–17, 18
*Return of the Vampire, The*, 21
rock musicals, 68, 70
romantic trend, 39, 46–48, 56

**S**
*Salem's Lot*, 36–37
Sangster, Jimmy, 22, 23
*Scars of Dracula*, 25
Schreck, Max, 12
shape-shifting, 39, 55, 62

silent movies, 8–12, **10**, **14**, 16, 20
*Son of Dracula* (1943), 21
*Son of Dracula* (1974), 68
Sookie Stackhouse (*True Blood*), 48
Stoker, Bram, 5–7, 13, 51
Straker (*Salem's Lot*), 36–37
*Suck*, 70
*Sundown*, 72
suspenseful science fiction, 59

**T**
television, 24, 30–31, 33, 36–37, 51, 65–67, **66**
*Thirst*, 74–75
*True Blood*, 48–49
*Twilight* series, 35, 38, 46–49, **49**, 54, **60**

**U**
*Underworld*, 45

**V**
vampire, history of the word, 7, 9
*Vampire's Kiss*, 65
*Vampires*, 62
*Vampyr*, 12, 14
*Van Helsing*, 45
Victoria Winters (*Dark Shadows*), 30
Vlad the Impaler/Tepes/Dracul, 5

**W**
Westerns, 72, 74
Whedon, Joss, 65–67